Month by Month
with Mary

Month by Month with Mary

Spiritual Insights for Marian Devotion

By Guido Gandolfo, SSP

Pauline
BOOKS & MEDIA
Boston

Library of Congress Cataloging-in-Publication Data 2019950178
CIP data on file.

ISBN 10: 0-8198-5014-4
ISBN 13: 978-0-8198-5014-0

Cover design by Rosana Usselmann

Cover art by Sassoferrato

Translated by John di Camillo

Published by Pauline Books & Media, 50 Saint Pauls Avenue, Boston, MA 02130-3491

Printed in the U.S.A.

www.pauline.org

Pauline Books & Media is the publishing house of the Daughters of St. Paul, an international congregation of women religious serving the Church with the communications media.

1 2 3 4 5 6 7 8 9   24 23 22 21 20

Contents

Foreword

"Jesus does not want us to walk alone, without a mother."

These words of Father Guido sum up his intentions in writing this small but intense volume on Mary: to live the year, to live our life with Mary—walking with our mother, walking with Jesus.

I am very happy to recommend Father Guido Gandolfo's book of spiritual insights for Marian devotion. I have known Father Guido for more than three decades, have had him as a retreat director, and have been spiritually enriched by his homilies on many occasions. Father Guido is a member of the Society of Saint Paul, one of the congregations that make up the Pauline Family, founded by Blessed James Alberione.

A renowned retreat director among members of the Pauline Family, Father Guido has traveled to many countries to share his spiritual wisdom and the treasure of Pauline spirituality. His own devotion to Mary, nurtured by the teaching of Blessed James Alberione, the Fathers of the Church, and the popes of our times is very evident in this volume. It's also contagious. I felt my own desire to know Mary more intimately increasing with every chapter.

That's what these reflections are meant to do: lead the reader into a deeper personal meditation on Mary's role in the Incarnation of Jesus in God's plan of salvation, and also on her role in the transformation of each one of us. For devotion to Mary always leads us to an even closer relationship with her Son, Jesus Christ.

This book is not only delightful in the way it is arranged—a Marian reflection for every month of the year, reminding us that Mary is always by our side—but it is also unique in some of its considerations. Besides reflections on liturgical Marian feasts and apparitions, Gandolfo offers compelling insights into Mary: as a prophetess in an interior and mystical sense, on what it means to *listen* like Mary, on the intimacy of Mary and Joseph, on Mary's role in the paschal mystery, on Mary as a teacher of prayer and as a temple of silence, the joy of the Trinity, the Star of the New Evangelization, and more. Thus, this book contains much material to renew and deepen one's own Marian devotion.

True to the heritage received from Blessed James Alberione, Father Guido shows us Mary not only as the Mother of Jesus, but also as his most perfect disciple. In this she is our model. "Every particle of Mary's person was shaped by the presence of the Son, the incarnate mercy of the Father," writes Father Guido. In Mary, "we become able to contemplate Jesus himself, the face of the Father's mercy."

Besides his own reflections and quotes from saints through the ages and popes of our times, Father Guido also intersperses his meditations with prayers that we, the readers, can make our own.

This little book is a great companion to another Marian title by a Pauline Family priest, Father Giuseppe Forlai, entitled *Mary, Mother of Apostles,* on how to live Marian devotion to proclaim Christ.

In Father Guido's words, "Mary will always remain with us and with the Church for all time, as dispenser of all graces and our most lovable mother. Thank you, Blessed Trinity, for this immense gift!"

MARY LEONORA WILSON, FSP

January 1, 2020
Feast of Mary, Mother of God

Preface

This book is the fruit of invaluable collaboration. Several years ago, Father Francesco Mariano Tadone, editor of the monthly periodical *Madre di Dio* (Mother of God), asked me to write a Marian contribution each month, offering some inspirational thoughts for the readers.

I eagerly accepted the invitation, as both a tribute of gratitude and love to the Mother and Queen of the apostles, and as a contribution to the Marian formation of the readers of *Madre di Dio*. Since the magazine is a publication of the Society of Saint Paul, it will be no surprise to find that excerpts from the authoritative writings of Louis-Marie Grignion de Montfort are accompanied by many citations drawn from the Marian spirituality of Blessed James Alberione, a priest and founder of the Pauline Family.

After four years of contributing to the periodical, various readers expressed their desire to have all of my

Marian commentaries in a handy little book. This led to the idea of revising my work so that the meditations might result in a book, which I happily offer to all those interested in letting Mary accompany them.

May we each feel over us the maternal protection of the Virgin Mary, our Mother, Teacher, and Queen of the Apostles.

Best wishes to all.

GUIDO GANDOLFO

Acknowledgments

The Scripture quotations contained herein are from the *New Revised Standard Version Bible: Catholic Edition,* copyright © 1989, 1993, Division of Christian Education of the National Council of the Churches of Christ in the United States of America. Used by permission. All rights reserved.

Excerpts from the English translation of the *Catechism of the Catholic Church* for use in the United States of America, copyright © 1994, United States Catholic Conference, Inc. — Libreria Editrice Vaticana. Used with permission.

Excerpts from *Mechthild of Hackeborn: The Book of Special Grace*, translated by Barbara Newman, Copyright © 2017 by Barbara Newman. Paulist Press, Inc., New York/Mahwah, NJ. Reprinted by permission of Paulist Press, Inc. www.paulistpress.com.

JANUARY

Mary, Mother of God

Peace and Blessings

January 1. We begin again: a new year, a new journey! Certainly we begin not with the resigned spirit of one who sees only the inevitable passing of time, but with the attitude of the believer who welcomes every new day as a renewed gift from God and intends to live them for the glory of the Giver.

At the beginning of the year, we are deluged with wishes through a variety of media: some sincere, others formal, and others trite. For us believers the most significant is the blessing of the Lord, which goes through Moses to Aaron and, in the Liturgy of the Word for today, reaches even us:

The LORD bless you and keep you;
the LORD make his face to shine upon you,
    and be gracious to you;
the LORD lift up his countenance upon you,
    and give you peace. (Nm 6:24–26)

Only God speaks the good and carries out the good. It is an efficacious wish that opens the heart to hope and does not disappoint us! Only in the filial relationship with the Father who blesses us will we be able to look to the future with trust: "To search the horizons of our life and our times, in watchful prayer; to peer into the night in order to recognize the fire that illuminates and guides, to gaze into the heavens, looking for the heralds of blessing for our dryness. To keep awake and watch, and to make intercession, firm in faith."[1]

With confidence we entrust the new year to Mary, that she may strengthen our fragile faith. We unite ourselves to the prayer addressed to her by consecrated men and women journeying in the footsteps of God: "You sustain our watching in the night, until the light of dawn anticipates the new day. Grant us a prophet's voice to tell the world about the joy of the Gospel, about

---

1. Congregation for Institutes of Consecrated Life and Societies of Apostolic Life, *Keep Watch! To Consecrated Men and Women Following in the Footsteps of God* (Vatican City: Libreria Editrice Vaticana–Pauline Publications Africa, 2014), no. 1, p. 8, https://cmswr.org/wp-content/uploads/Keep-Watch.pdf.

the blessedness of those who search the horizons of new lands and heavens (see Rev 21:1) and anticipate their presence in the human city. Help us to proclaim the fecundity of the Spirit under the banner of the essential and the small."[2]

At the beginning of the New Year, when the whole world is celebrating the World Day of Peace, let us recall that profound and passionate appeal of Paul VI in 1968, dedicating every January 1 to the celebration of the World Day of Peace:

> It is Our desire that then, every year, this commemoration be repeated as a hope and as a promise, at the beginning of the calendar which measures and outlines the path of human life in time, that peace with its just and beneficent equilibrium may dominate the development of events to come. . . . It is, therefore, to true peace, to just and balanced peace, in the sincere recognition of the rights of the human person and of the independence of the individual nations, that We invite men of wisdom and strength to dedicate this Day. . . .
>
> From the Gospel's precept to pardon and to have mercy, we can draw forces which will regenerate society.[3]

---

2. Ibid., no. 19, p. 64.

3. Paul VI, Message for the Observation of a Day of Peace, January 1, 1968, http://w2.vatican.va/content/paul-vi/en/messages/peace/documents/hf_p-vi_mes_19671208_i-world-day-for-peace.html.

Mother of God

The first day of the year is also gladdened by the radiant figure of Mary, the Mother of God. Mary's light shines brightly because it reflects the light of Christ, Son of the Most High and son of Mary. It fills us with renewed awe that God willed to raise this simple and humble woman of Nazareth to such a great height. Truly God looked with favor on the "lowly" condition of Mary (see Lk 1:48), raising her to the status of mother of his beloved Son!

Blessed James Alberione therefore comments:

> The Divine Motherhood of Mary is the font of all the graces and of all the privileges granted to her. . . . In Mary, the most intimate and highest union was fulfilled between creature and Creator; in her, the Word of God assumed human nature, hypostatically united with his divine person. Mary is raised to the highest dignity which borders on divinity. She is the *Mother of Love*.[4]

Three centuries earlier, supporting Alberione's mariological perspective on the dignity of Mary, Saint Louis-Marie Grignion de Montfort borrows the words of the Apostle Paul[5] as he writes:

---

4. James Alberione, "Le Feste di Maria Santissima" [The feasts of most holy Mary], in *Maria nostra speranza* [Mary, our hope] (Alba, CN: Pia Società Figlie di San Paolo, 1939), vol. II, pp. 236, 240.

5. See 1 Cor 2:9.

After that we must cry out with the Apostle, *Nec oculus vidit, nec auris audivit, nec in cor hominis ascendit* —"Eye has not seen, nor ear heard, nor man's heart comprehended"—the beauties, the grandeurs, the excellences, of Mary, the miracle of the miracles of grace, of nature, and of glory.

If you wish to understand the Mother, says a saint, understand the Son; for she is the worthy Mother of God. *Hic taceat omnis lingua*—"Here let every tongue be silent."[6]

What tenderness Mary must have shown to Jesus, the son given to her by the heavenly Father; and how it must have been reciprocated by Jesus, a son so docile and so affectionate!

Having contemplated the profound mystery of Emmanuel (God with us), let us now pause to contemplate the beauty of the Virgin Mother, allowing ourselves to be guided by the prayer that Dante puts on the lips of Saint Bernard in the *Divine Comedy*:

Thou Virgin Mother, daughter of thy Son,
Humble and high beyond all other creature,
The limit fixed of the eternal counsel,
Thou art the one who such nobility

---

6. Louis-Marie Grignion de Montfort, *A Treatise on the True Devotion to the Blessed Virgin*, trans. Frederick William Faber (London: Burns and Lambert, 1863), 6.

To human nature gave, that its Creator
Did not disdain to make himself its creature.[7]

Let us joyfully celebrate the feast of the motherhood of Mary: a unique wonder of God's omnipotence. Jesus was brought into the world by Mary, and it is she who presented him to Joseph, the shepherds, the Magi, and then to the whole world. "Mother": who knows how many times Jesus would have uttered this sweet title when addressing her? "What sweetness must have entered into Mary's heart when hearing herself called Mother by the Incarnate Son of God! And on the other hand, what an act of humility on the part of Jesus!"[8]

For this reason, our heart is filled with great confidence. Although aware that the social and political landscape is rather disturbing, and mindful that there are reasons for uneasiness even on the ecclesial level, we believers do not allow ourselves to be overcome by discouragement. Our confidence and our assurance are in the Mother who knows our problems, defends us from dangers, and will lead us to safe ground.

---

7. Dante Alighieri, *The Divine Comedy*, trans. Henry Wadsworth Longfellow, Paradise XXXIII, nos. 1–6, Project Gutenberg EText, http://www.gutenberg.org/cache/epub/1004/pg1004-images.html.   Original Italian: "Vergine Madre, figlia del tuo figlio, / umile e alta più che creatura, / termine fisso d'etterno consiglio, / tu se' colei che l'umana natura / nobilitasti sì, che 'l suo fattore / non disdegnò di farsi sua fattura."

8. James Alberione, *Per un rinnovamento spirituale* [Toward a spiritual renewal] (Cinisello Balsamo, Italy: San Paolo, 2006), 263.

Mary, the Prophetess

The Gospel passage proposed for the first day of the year recounts the journey made by the shepherds, after receiving the angel's invitation (see Lk 2:9–11), to visit and contemplate the child Jesus. They found Mary, Joseph, and the baby lying in the manger, and related everything that had been told to them about the child. And then, as Luke the Evangelist states, "Mary kept all these things, reflecting on them in her heart" (Lk 2:19). In an article published in 1989 with the title "You Are Full of Grace,"[9] Cardinal Joseph Ratzinger, later Pope Benedict XVI, highlighted the contemplative nature of Mary's prayer and the mystical aspect of her being, which the Church Fathers liken to the prophetic. In pondering all those things (see Lk 2:19, 51: facts and events), Mary knows how to receive the Word, which creates meaning and fills every event. Mary's meditative attitude challenges the Church and each of us, especially at the beginning of a new year of spiritual and apostolic life. From Mary emerges the figure of the pious Israelite of the Old Testament as described in Psalm 119, who loves the word of God, carries it in his heart, reflects on it, meditates on it day and night, and is totally permeated

---

9. See Joseph Ratzinger, "You Are Full of Grace: Elements of Biblical Devotion to Mary," *Communio* 16.1 (Spring 1989): 54–68.

with it. The Fathers of the Church summarized all of this in a beautiful and expressive image articulated by Theodotus of Ancyra: "The Virgin has given birth, the prophetess has given birth. Mary the prophetess, through listening, conceived the living God. Indeed, the natural path of the word is listening" (*Homily* 4).

Divine motherhood and constant openness to the word of God are here considered intimately united: listening attentively to the angel's greeting, she welcomes the Holy Spirit into herself. Mary fully welcomes the Word, which in her becomes the understanding of prophetic reality and splendor of truth, which sheds light on the present moment open to the future.

Mary's motherhood is closely related to her profound capacity to listen to the Word. A very enlightening perspective for the new year!

The then-Cardinal Ratzinger highlighted two fundamental aspects of Marian listening:

a) *listening to the Word in its generative dimension*. Mary welcomes the Word so completely that it becomes flesh in her. Listening attentively and lovingly brings fruit, opens new perspectives, and becomes a gift. In this environment the Spirit enters and gives rise to a new creation. Otherwise, it would remain sterile and ineffectual hearing!

b) *listening to the Word in its prophetic dimension*. Perhaps we are not very familiar with the idea of Mary as a prophetess, in an interior and mystical sense, but this was not the case for the Church Fathers. Prophetic listening enables the believer to live in the splendor of truth. The truth that God gives us, if well-guarded by the heart, ensures the only valid explanation of the present and even offers the authentic direction open to the future.[10] And the subject of Christian mysticism even remains open. What wonderful insights for the new year the benevolence of the Trinity allows us to welcome in order to begin a brand-new journey!

---

10. See Michele G. Masciarelli, *Il segno della donna: Maria nella teologia di Joseph Ratzinger* [Sign of the woman: Mary in the theology of Joseph Ratzinger] (Cinisello Balsamo, Italy: San Paolo, 2007), 79–88.

Mary, Who Gives Jesus to the World

Model of Consecrated Life

Forty days after Christmas (February 2) we celebrate the Presentation of Jesus in the Temple. In accordance with the Law of Moses, Mary and Joseph bring Jesus to Jerusalem (see Lk 2:22). Mary presents Jesus in the Temple to offer him to the Lord and introduce him into the people of Israel. This is perhaps the role most suited to her: the mother who gives Jesus. Even today, as Blessed James Alberione would say, the Mother of God continues to give Jesus to the world and does so even through each one of us. The mission of the Church is always to bring and give Jesus to all!

On February 2, the universal Church celebrates the World Day of Consecrated Life. Lifting up our prayer, we too ask the Virgin Mary, together with John Paul II, to sustain all consecrated men and women:

> Mary, image of the Church, the Bride without spot or wrinkle, which by imitating you "preserves with virginal purity an integral faith, a firm hope, and a sincere charity," sustain consecrated persons on their journey toward the sole and eternal Blessedness.
>
> To you, Virgin of the Visitation, do we entrust them, that they may go forth to meet human needs, to bring help, but above all to bring Jesus. Teach them to proclaim the mighty things which the Lord accomplishes in the world, that all peoples may extol the greatness of his name. Support them in their work for the poor, the hungry, those without hope, the little ones, and all who seek your Son with a sincere heart. To you, our Mother, who desire the spiritual and apostolic renewal of your sons and daughters in a response of love and complete dedication to Christ, we address our confident prayer. You who did the will of the Father, ever ready in obedience, courageous in poverty, and receptive in fruitful virginity, obtain from your divine Son that all who have received the gift of following him in the consecrated life may be enabled to bear witness to that gift by their transfigured lives, as they joyfully make their way with all their brothers and sisters toward our heavenly homeland and the light which will never grow dim. We ask you this, that in everyone and in everything glory, adoration,

and love may be given to the Most High Lord of all things, who is Father, Son, and Holy Spirit.[1]

Two petitions seem to emerge from this prayer of John Paul II. The first is the request that the Pope himself addresses to Mary, that consecrated persons may always "proclaim the mighty things that the Lord accomplishes." Even Pope Francis, in his apostolic letter *To All Consecrated People* published on the occasion of the Year of Consecrated Life, repeatedly called for "following in the footsteps of past generations in order to grasp the high ideals, and the vision and values which inspired them, beginning with the founders and foundresses and the first communities."[2]

The second petition that emerges from John Paul II's prayer highlights the value of witness, that those who have received "the gift of following him [Christ] in the consecrated life may be enabled to bear witness to that gift by their transfigured lives." That which constitutes the identity of a consecrated person becomes in this way an invocation to the Virgin: "conforming one's

1. John Paul II, Apostolic Exhortation *Vita Consecrata*, March 25, 1996, no. 112, http://w2.vatican.va/content/john-paul-ii/en/apost_exhortations/documents/hf_jp-ii_exh_25031996_vita-consecrata.html.

2. Francis, Apostolic Exhortation *To All Consecrated People*, November 21, 2014, pt. I, no. 1, http://w2.vatican.va/content/john-paul-ii/en/apost_exhortations/documents/hf_jp-ii_exh_25031996_vita-consecrata.html.

whole existence" to Christ should lead to a "profound 'configuration' to the mystery of Christ."[3] Imagine how Blessed Alberione's heart would have throbbed to hear expressions so lofty and so much in harmony with his thinking! Pope Francis took this same perspective, wishing to dedicate a year as a valuable opportunity "for bearing vigorous and joyful witness before the world to the holiness and vitality present in so many of those called to follow Jesus in the consecrated life."[4]

Our Lady of Lourdes

The month of February gives us another day dear to every Christian: the remembrance of the first apparition of the Blessed Virgin at Lourdes on February 11, 1858. Four years earlier, Pope Pius IX had proclaimed the dogma of the Immaculate Conception of Mary. The definitive pronouncement by the Pope had closed a period of intense debate over this truth and "placed a supernatural seal on what the faithful already held as certain, because it was defined by the Vicar of Christ."[5] The supernatural quality of the apparitions (recognized

---

3. See John Paul II, *Vita Consecrata*, no. 16.
4. Francis, Apostolic Exhortation *To All Consecrated People*, November 21, 2014, pt. I, no. 1.
5. See James Alberione, *Maria nostra speranza* [Mary, our hope], vol. II (Alba, CN: Pia Società Figlie di San Paolo, 1939), 47.

by the Church only four years after their occurrence) was confirmed by a series of extraordinary wonders and miracles: infirmities of every kind were healed at Lourdes.

It is a phenomenon that confirms, yesterday and still today, the overwhelming goodness of Mary who is ready to intervene so that all may return to her Son through conversion of life and the healing of their infirmities. As a loving mother, Mary did not intend to remain far away from us, relegated to the heavens and exalted by the angels and saints, but wished to visit us, appearing multiple times and in different places. All of her visits were directed to invite men and women to look to heaven and to live so as to attain eternal salvation. On the liturgical memorial of the apparition of the Blessed Virgin Mary, it is a tradition that the World Day of the Sick is celebrated at Lourdes. Its objective is to enable us "to understand the deep love of God for every human being, especially those afflicted by sickness or pain,"[6] as affirmed by Benedict XVI on the occasion of the Twenty-First World Day of the Sick at the Marian shrine of Altötting (the Catholic heart of Bavaria). With the eyes and the heart of Mary, each of us can have a greater attentiveness and compassionate understanding toward

---

6. Benedict XVI, Message for the Twenty-First World Day of the Sick (February 11, 2013), January 2, 2013, http://w2.vatican.va/content/benedict-xvi/en/messages/sick/documents/hf_ben-xvi_mes_20130102_world-day-of-the-sick-2013.html.

every person, especially the weak, the suffering, and those who need help.

Mary, Hope of the World

Let us now turn to Mary with confidence, that she may keep motherly watch over the nations of the world, and reflect on Saint John Paul II's prayer:

Mary, Mother of hope,
accompany us on our journey!
Teach us to proclaim the living God;
help us to bear witness to Jesus,
the one Savior;
make us kindly toward our neighbors,
welcoming to the needy,
concerned for justice,
impassioned builders of a more just world;
intercede for us
as we carry out our work in history,
certain that the Father's plan will be fulfilled. . . .

Watch over all Christians:
may they advance confidently
on the path of unity,
as a leaven of harmony.
Watch over young people:
the hope of the future,
may they respond with generosity
to the call of Jesus.

Watch over the leaders of nations:
may they be committed
to building a common house
which respects the dignity and rights
of every person.
Mary, *give us Jesus!*
Grant that we may follow him and love him!
He is the hope of the Church,
... and of all humanity![7]

The Virgin Mary is invoked primarily as the "mother of hope," who sustains our weak hope. The Pope directs to her his supplication on our behalf: walk with us, be at our side, accompany us every step of the way. Mary is asked to teach us to be authentic witnesses capable of proclaiming the living God, affirming with conviction that Jesus, her son, is the only Savior. It is in this manner that we are all invited to be attentive toward our brothers and sisters, with a welcoming attitude especially toward those who find themselves in need, so that we may become true workers of justice. Mary's presence and work within us will lead us to become "impassioned builders of a more just world." It will be the Virgin herself who intercedes on our behalf, while we offer our small but indispensable

---

7. John Paul II, Post-Synodal Apostolic Exhortation *Ecclesia in Europa*, June 28, 2003, no. 125, http://w2.vatican.va/content/john-paul-ii/en/apost_exhortations/documents/hf_jp-ii_exh_20030628_ecclesia-in-europa.html.

contribution to building the beautiful story of each day, fully convinced "that the Father's plan will be fulfilled."

For the leaders of nations, we ask that they be "committed to building a common house which respects the dignity and rights of every person." All this is on the condition that each person may joyfully set out to follow Jesus, Mary's son. He alone is and always remains "the hope of the Church, and of all humanity." He already lives with us and among us, and indeed within us!

MARCH

Mary, Full of Grace

The Servant of the Lord

The month of March approaches enveloped in the light of the sun, which progressively brightens and warms our days, and in the spiritual light that flows from the liturgical celebrations. Among these, the Annunciation of the Lord stands out. This feast, dear to the Church and to all believers, invites us to pause and meditate on the moment in which the Most Blessed Trinity encounters humanity and initiates redemption, through the immeasurable gift of the Incarnation of Jesus. A young girl from Nazareth, named Mary, was chosen to be the mother of Jesus, the Savior. Mary, filled with divine favor, made "full of grace" (*kecharitomene*, Lk 1:28), responds to the divine invitation of the angel Gabriel with a simple and humble, "Here am I." How could she have answered differently, she who declares herself the servant of the Lord (see Lk 1:38)?

The Holy Spirit, who is infinitely pleased with her, will proclaim her "blessed" (happy) through the mouth of Elizabeth, and will add a new name: "she who believed" (in Greek, *he pisteusasa*, the believer, Lk 1:45)! What greater gift could we receive from an anxious but decisive "yes"?

Looking at Mary, we ask ourselves: What is the value today (for us and for those around us) of the many "yeses" by which we allow God to carry out his Word?

In this regard, Blessed Alberione comments: "From all eternity God has marked out a path for every creature, and he marked one especially for Mary; he provided her with suitable gifts of nature and grace. Every person should follow their divine calling, if they want divine blessings. . . . Blessed are the children who follow the desires of the heavenly Father!"[1]

The feast of the Annunciation often falls in the heart of Lent. What better opportunity to "follow the desires of the heavenly Father" than with Mary's example? Lent prepares us to participate in the fruits of the passion,

---

1. James Alberione, *Brevi meditazioni per ogni giorno dell'anno* [Brief meditations for every day of the year] (Cinisello Balsamo, Italy: San Paolo, 2008), 365.

death, and resurrection of Jesus with a serious journey of conversion and renewal of spirit. We welcome this special season as a precious gift, according to an image dear to Father Alberione, who reminds us that "Lent is like a great retreat made by Christians all over the world, who prepare themselves for new life and resurrection in Christ."[2]

Pope Francis urges us to always test every thought, desire, or action, to discern and identify the path of Jesus:

> If a thought or desire takes you along the path of humility, of selflessness, of serving others, it is the path of Jesus; but if it takes you along the path of conceit, vanity, or pride, or along the path to abstract thinking it is not the path of Jesus. The temptations that Jesus himself had to undergo in the desert confirm this. All three of the propositions . . . sought to lead Jesus away from the path of service, humility, and charity he accomplished by his life.[3]

Saint Joseph

The feast of Saint Joseph sheds a new light on our reflection.

---

2. Alberione, *Brevi meditazioni*, 571.

3. Francis, Morning Meditation in the Chapel of the *Domus Sanctae Marthae*, January 7, 2014 (translation John A. Di Camillo). Summary available at https://w2.vatican.va/content/francesco/en/cotidie/2014/documents/papa-francesco-cotidie_20140207_first-galilee.html.

Joseph is a man of deep faith: silent, obedient, strong in the face of difficulty, a relational man. He trusted Mary, guarding in his heart and daily living the mystery entrusted to him. The spiritual masters have always emphasized that intimacy with Mary and familiarity with Jesus were gifts granted to Joseph by Providence. He surely will not fail to intercede for each of us to obtain the same divine gifts. As Blessed Alberione commented, referring to the words of Saint Louis-Marie Grignion de Montfort, "The soul that loves Mary with a confident love advances more in one month than other souls with years of effort who do not love Mary."[4]

In other words, with an intense love for Mary we make great progress in holiness. And rapid progress! From Mary and Joseph, we too learn familiarity and loving dialogue with Jesus. We learn of an intimacy that will bring us to think more and more like Jesus, to work like Jesus, and like Jesus to make a gift of ourselves to our brothers and sisters, until it becomes Jesus himself who lives and communicates through us! Saint John Paul II's apostolic exhortation *Redemptoris Custos* outlines very clearly the figure of Joseph, the earthly father of Jesus and true spouse of the Virgin Mary: "Just as Saint Joseph took loving care of Mary and gladly dedicated

---

4. Alberione, *Per un rinnovamento spirituale*, 446.

himself to Jesus Christ's upbringing, he likewise watches over and protects Christ's Mystical Body, that is, the Church, of which the Virgin Mary is the exemplar and model."[5]

The human story of Joseph seemed to unfold as did that of many young men of his age. For some time, he had been fascinated by Mary's transparent beauty, and Joseph had been bound to her by betrothal (legal marriage). But before going to live together, the lives of Mary and Joseph were visited by a completely unexpected event: Mary's virginal conception through the power of the Holy Spirit.

The young man was greatly troubled and his decision to send Mary away secretly was impressive. At this point the heavenly Father intervened through the voice of an angel (see Mt 1:18-24).

> There is a strict parallel between the "annunciation" in Matthew's text and the one in Luke. *The divine messenger introduces Joseph to the mystery of Mary's motherhood.* While remaining a virgin, she who by law is his "spouse" has become a mother through the power of the Holy Spirit. And when the Son in Mary's womb comes into the world, he must receive the name Jesus.

---

5. John Paul II, Apostolic Exhortation *Redemptoris Custos*, August 15, 1989, no. 1, http://w2.vatican.va/content/john-paul-ii/en/apost_exhortations/documents/hf_jp-ii_exh_15081989_redemptoris-custos.html.

This was a name known among the Israelites and sometimes given to their sons. In this case, however, *it is the Son who,* in accordance with the divine promise, *will bring to perfect fulfillment the meaning of the name Jesus—Yehos ua'*—which means *"God saves."*

Joseph is visited by *the messenger* as "Mary's spouse," as the one who in due time must give this name to the Son to be born of the Virgin of Nazareth who is married to him. It is *to Joseph,* then, that the messenger turns, *entrusting to him the responsibilities of an earthly father regarding Mary's Son.*

"When Joseph woke from sleep, he did as the angel of the Lord commanded him and took Mary as his wife" (see Mt 1:24). He took her in all the mystery of her motherhood. He took her together with the Son who had come into the world by the power of the Holy Spirit. In this way he *showed a readiness of will like Mary's* regarding what God asked of him through the angel. . . .

Now at the beginning of this pilgrimage, *the faith of Mary meets the faith of Joseph.* If Elizabeth said of the Redeemer's Mother, "blessed is she who believed," in a certain sense this blessedness can be referred to Joseph as well, since he responded positively to the word of God when it was communicated to him at the decisive moment. While it is true that Joseph did not respond to the angel's "announcement" in the same way as Mary, he "*did* as the angel of the Lord commanded him and took his wife." *What he did is the clearest "obedience of faith"* (see Rom 1:5; 16:26; 2 Cor 10:5–6).[6]

If it is important to profess the virginal conception of Jesus, it is just as important to defend Mary's marriage to Joseph. The son of Mary is also the son of Joseph by virtue of the marriage bond that unites Mary and Joseph.

John Paul II underscores that Joseph's virtue of industriousness was an admirable example and played a notable part in the human development of Jesus "in wisdom, age and grace" (see Lk 2:52). His work was always carried out in silence and reached the highest degree of contemplation.

Finally, the Pope recalls that Saint Joseph is the patron of the universal Church. Therefore, the Pope considers this popular invocation always relevant: "Graciously assist us from heaven in our struggle with the powers of darkness and just as once you saved the Child Jesus from mortal danger, so now defend God's holy Church from the snares of her enemies and from all adversity."[7]

---

6. John Paul II, *Redemptoris Custos*, nos. 3–4.

7. Ibid., no. 31, citing Leo XIII, "Prayer to St. Joseph," immediately after the text of his encyclical letter *Quamquam Pluries* (August 15, 1889), http://w2.vatican.va/content/leo-xiii/en/encyclicals/documents/hf_l-xiii_enc_15081889_quamquam-pluries.html: "Aid us from on high, most valiant defender, in this conflict with the powers of darkness. And even as of old you did rescue the Child Jesus from the peril of his life, so now defend God's Holy Church from the snares of the enemy and from all adversity."

The Annunciation of the Incarnation

The mystery of the Incarnation which we contemplate every March 25 (when there are no changes in the liturgical calendar) is so great and so holy that one is almost afraid to comment on it. It is better to approach this topic through the reflections of the saints and the words of the Church.

> God the Father has not given his only-begotten to the world except through Mary. Whatever sighs the patriarchs may have sent forth, whatever prayers the prophets and the saints of the old law may have offered up to obtain that treasure for four thousand years, it was only Mary who merited it; it was only Mary who found grace before God by the force of her prayers and the eminence of her virtues.[8]

Even the Council Fathers did not fail to meditate and comment on the words of the angel Gabriel to Mary:

> Adorned from the first instant of her conception with the radiance of an entirely unique holiness, the Virgin of Nazareth is greeted, on God's command, by an angel messenger as "full of grace" (see Lk 1:28), and to the heavenly messenger she replies: "Behold the hand-maid of the Lord, be it done unto me according to thy

---

8. De Montfort, *True Devotion*, pt. I, sec. I, p. 8.

word" (see Lk 1:38). Thus Mary, a daughter of Adam, consenting to the divine Word, became the mother of Jesus, the one and only Mediator. Embracing God's salvific will with a full heart and impeded by no sin, she devoted herself totally as a handmaid of the Lord to the person and work of her Son, under him and with him, by the grace of almighty God, serving the mystery of redemption.[9]

For his part, Blessed James Alberione wisely highlights Mary's willingness:

As soon as Mary realized with certainty that God was speaking to her through the angel, she was ready like the handmaid who depends on her Lord for everything. With readiness and generosity, she accomplished the divine will in everything for her entire life.[10]

This leads to a starting point for our examination:

Does God find me always ready to follow his wishes? Even if mysterious and painful for me? Do I seek my will or the divine will?[11]

9. Second Vatican Council, Dogmatic Constitution *Lumen Gentium*, November 21, 1964, no. 56, http://www.vatican.va/archive/hist_councils/ii_vatican_council/documents/vat-ii_const_19641121_lumen-gentium_en.html.

10. Alberione, *Brevi meditazioni*, 365.

11. Ibid.

Mary, Our Hope

The heartbreaking and salvific events of the passion, death, and resurrection of Jesus did not find Mary absent—to the contrary! Jesus had already united her so intimately to his mission, and he wanted her joined to him even more closely in the final days of his earthly life. In that circumstance Mary fully reveals herself as Co-Redemptrix: "Jesus sacrificed his flesh, Mary sacrificed her soul."[12] In her, hope did not die, as Benedict XVI wrote in his encyclical letter *Spe Salvi*. In this month, it can be of great light and spiritual comfort to revisit the touching prayer to Mary at the conclusion of that papal document:

> Holy Mary, you belonged to the humble and great souls of Israel who, like Simeon, were "looking for the consolation of Israel" (Lk 2:25) and hoping, like Anna, "for the redemption of Jerusalem" (Lk 2:38). Your life was thoroughly imbued with the sacred scriptures of Israel which spoke of hope, of the promise made to Abraham and his descendants (see Lk 1:55). . . . But alongside the joy which, with your *Magnificat*, you proclaimed in word and song for all the centuries to hear, you also knew the dark sayings of the prophets about

---

12. James Alberione, *Maria Regina degli Apostoli* [Mary, Queen of Apostles] (Cinisello Balsamo, Italy: San Paolo, 2008), 96.

the suffering of the servant of God in this world. . . .
In this way you saw the growing power of hostility and
rejection which built up around Jesus until the hour
of the Cross, when you had to look upon the Savior
of the world, the heir of David, the Son of God dying
like a failure, exposed to mockery, between criminals.
Then you received the word of Jesus: "Woman, behold,
your Son!" (Jn 19:26). From the Cross you received
a new mission. From the Cross you became a mother
in a new way: the mother of all those who believe in
your Son Jesus and wish to follow him. The sword
of sorrow pierced your heart. Did hope die? Did the
world remain definitively without light, and life without purpose? . . . No, at the foot of the Cross, on the
strength of Jesus' own word, you became the mother
of believers. In this faith, which even in the darkness
of Holy Saturday bore the certitude of hope, you made
your way toward Easter morning. . . . The "kingdom" of
Jesus was not as might have been imagined. It began in
that hour, and of this "kingdom" there will be no end.
Thus, you remain in the midst of the disciples as their
Mother, as the Mother of hope. Holy Mary, Mother
of God, our Mother, teach us to believe, to hope, to
love with you. Show us the way to his Kingdom! Star
of the Sea, shine upon us and guide us on our way![13]

13. Benedict XVI, Encyclical Letter *Spe Salvi*, November 30, 2007, no. 50, http://w2.vatican.va/content/benedict-xvi/en/encyclicals/docu-ments/hf_ben-xvi_enc_20071130_spe-salvi.html.

In this prayer we can hear the heart of Pope Benedict XVI resound for the Virgin Mary, contemplated in her difficult pilgrimage of faith. That path of trustful hope in the Father, set in motion by an angel's words, "Do not be afraid, Mary" (Lk 1:30), reaches the summit of heroism on Calvary, when according to John Paul II's expression, she was "the witness, humanly speaking, of the *complete negation*"[14] of the angel's promises: "He will be great, and will be called the Son of the Most High, and the Lord God will give to him the throne of his ancestor David.... And of his kingdom there will be no end" (Lk 1:32–33).

When would that kingdom be manifested? "Could it have ended before it began? No, at the foot of the Cross, on the strength of Jesus' own word, you became the mother of believers. In this faith, which even in the darkness of Holy Saturday bore the certitude of hope, you made your way toward Easter morning.... The 'kingdom' of Jesus was not as might have been imagined."[15]

With heroic faith, Mary entrusted herself and believed: "She believed the angel's word without hesitation, and believed it faithfully and constantly up to the foot of the Cross."[16]

---

14. John Paul II, Encyclical Letter *Redemptoris Mater*, March 25, 1987, no. 18, http://w2.vatican.va/content/john-paul-ii/en/encyclicals/documents/hf_jp-ii_enc_25031987_redemptoris-mater.html.

15. Benedict XVI, *Spe Salvi*, no. 50.

16. De Montfort, *True Devotion*, pt. II, sec. IV, no. 2, p. 181.

Mary, the Woman of Easter

The Mother Who Bears Life in Suffering

In our Marian reflection, the irreplaceable role of the mother of Jesus in the preparation and fulfillment of the passion requires our close attention.

Blessed Alberione invites us to pause and meditate, especially about Good Friday:

How painful that day must have been for Mary! Enlightened by the Scriptures and the preaching of her divine Son, Mary knew that the time had come for the ancient sacrifice to be abolished. She knew that the time had come for him to be sacrificed for the redemption of humanity. If Jesus went to Gethsemane, what would Mary have done but pray? When Jesus was captured, when he was condemned, during the terrible night that the divine Redeemer spent in the hands of the soldiers, during Peter's denials, where would Mary have been? If her beloved was suffering, she was surely keeping vigil in prayer. Mary chose the shortest path to reach her Son and accompany him to Calvary. The time has come: she is there, stronger than Abraham in offering her Son to the heavenly Father. Who could possibly describe Mary's torments? She is crucified with her Son; the nails driven through Jesus' hands and feet pierce her heart. What suffering for her to see the agony of him who is her whole life! What suffering in seeing her Jesus take his last breath on the Cross![1]

We seem to hear once again the poignant sermon of Saint Bernard:

Truly, blessed Mother, a sword has pierced your soul. For unless it had, it would not have penetrated the flesh of your Son. And after your Jesus—he is everyone's, but especially yours—has sent out his spirit, the cruel lance, not sparing him even after death, although it could harm him no more, opens his side, and while it clearly cannot touch his soul, it pierces yours. Without a doubt his soul was not there, but clearly yours could not be wrenched away. Yes, a violent grief pierced your soul, so that we may say with good reason that you are more than a martyr, in that your feeling of compassion exceeded physical suffering.

---

1. See Alberione, *Maria nostra speranza*, vol. II, 76–77.

Did not these words wound you more than a sword, truly piercing your soul, reaching even to the division of soul and spirit: "Woman, behold your son"? What a substitution! John will be to you as Jesus, the son of Zebedee in place of the Son of Man, a man pure and simple instead of the true God! When you heard this, how could it not pierce your most affectionate soul when ours, although of stone, although of iron, are torn by its very description?[2]

The contemplation of this mystery also resounded in the heart of Saint Louis-Marie Grignion de Montfort:

God-made-man has found his liberty in seeing himself imprisoned in her womb. He has made his omnipotence shine forth in letting himself be carried by that Blessed Virgin. He has found his glory and his Father's in hiding his splendors from all creatures here below and revealing them to Mary only. He has glorified his independence and his majesty, in depending on that sweet Virgin, in his conception, in his birth, in his presentation in the temple, in his hidden life of thirty years, and even in his death, where she was to be present, in order that he might make with her but one same sacrifice, and be immolated to the Eternal

---

2. "Sunday within the Octave of the Assumption," in Bernard of Clairvaux, *Sermons for the Autumn Season*, trans. Irene Edmonds, ed. Mark Scott, Cistercian Fathers Series 54 (Collegeville, MN: Liturgical Press / Cistercian Publications, 2016), nos. 14–15, p. 68.

Father by her consent; just as Isaac of old was offered by Abraham's consent to the will of God. It is she who nourished him, supported him, brought him up, and then sacrificed him for us.[3]

Mary does not complain, but with complete submission accepts the will of God. What an example for us! Let us turn our shared prayer for all people to Mary, Mother of Sorrows, that all may be touched by the fruits of redemption and attain eternal salvation.

Co-Redemptrix

In its liturgical and spiritual aspect, the month of April is especially enriched by the Pasch of the Lord. The preceding weeks constitute a fruitful journey of ascendance toward that event. With the celebration of the passion, death, and resurrection of Jesus, Holy Week is the heart of the entire liturgical year. The long day of Easter, lasting an entire week, is intended to prolong among the faithful the alleluia and the joy of the resurrection.

What is Mary's role in the paschal mystery? Undoubtedly very significant, indeed essential. Writers of spiritual theology have always recognized Mary, the

---

3. De Montfort, *True Devotion*, pt. I, sec. I, p. 9.

mother of Jesus, as the "co-redemptrix." While not using this term, the Second Vatican Council nonetheless took up its content. The role of co-redemptrix filled Mary's life, from the birth of Jesus to his passion, preparing and predisposing all things with a view to its fulfillment. The fundamental moment is enveloped in the "here am I" she voiced to the angel (see Lk 1:38), the "yes" that enabled the Son of God to come into the world and accomplish his mission. Various authors affirm that even if Mary's work had been limited to that consent, already it would have been sufficient to consider her as co-redemptrix because of her mediation for the salvation of all.[4] With what intensity Mary became aware of what it meant for Jesus (and for herself) to "be in my Father's house" (Lk 2:49)! With what delicacy she went about raising the young Jesus, for his sublime and anguished mission! The role of "co-redemptrix" involved Mary above all in the fulfillment of Jesus' hour: the great moment foretold by the Scriptures. Blessed Alberione contemplates the time of the offering in this way:

> A reciprocal gaze of tender love between Mother and Son was enough to understand one another, to unite themselves in suffering, intention, and sacrifice. . . .

---

4. See Saint Alphonsus, Pius IX, Leo XIII, Pius X. See James Alberione, *Mary Queen of Apostles* (Jamaica Plain, MA: Daughters of St. Paul, 1976), 104–06.

There were many women, but the Virgin had an entirely unique task: she was the co-redemptrix of the human race. She offered the Son; she offered herself. Two altars: a Cross for the Son, a heart pierced by a sharp sword for Mary.[5]

The Mother's sacrifice was a prolonged martyrdom, because she always contemplated in her spirit the passion of her son for the salvation of the world. There is no doubt that every suffering of Jesus was reflected in her heart: the abandonment, the betrayal, the scourging, the thorns, and the pain of the nails.

Pope Francis affirms that at the crucifixion Jesus "could feel at his feet the consoling presence of his mother and his friend."[6] And in recounting the dialogue that occurred between them (see Jn 19:26–27), the Pope gives us a truly moving reflection:

These words of the dying Jesus are not chiefly the expression of his devotion and concern for his mother; rather, they are a revelatory formula which manifests the mystery of a special saving mission. Jesus left us his mother to be our mother. Only after doing so did

---

5. Alberione, *Brevi meditazioni*, 386.

6. Pope Francis, Apostolic Exhortation *Evangelii Gaudium*, November 24, 2013, no. 285, http://w2.vatican.va/content/francesco/en/apost_exhortations/documents/papa-francesco_esortazione-ap_20131124_evangelii-gaudium.html.

Jesus know that "all was now finished" (Jn 19:28). At the foot of the cross, at the supreme hour of the new creation, Christ led us to Mary. He brought us to her because he did not want us to journey without a mother, and our people read in this maternal image all the mysteries of the Gospel.[7]

Jesus does not want us to walk alone, without a mother. The Belgian Jesuit and Scripture scholar Cornelius à Lapide, cited by Alberione, has some very incisive words about this: "O immense goodness of Jesus! He willed that his mother outlive him on this earth to assist the Church, that in his place she should be a solid pillar, a doctor of the apostles and the consolation of the faithful."[8]

The Gospels do not speak of an appearance of the risen Lord to his mother, but tradition and the heart persuade us that he did indeed appear to her on the first day of the week. He who had joined her to himself from the incarnation to the passion, surely must have reserved for her a joyful appearance when risen. Mary will always remain with us and with the Church for all time, as dispenser of all graces and our most lovable mother. Thank you, Blessed Trinity, for this immense gift!

---

7. Ibid.
8. Cornelius à Lapide, cited in James Alberione, *Mary Queen of Apostles*, 149.

The Mother of Mercy

The feast of Divine Mercy offers us a framework to reflect on Mary as the Mother of Mercy. As Pope Francis affirms, it is "the sweetness of her countenance" that attracts all people, especially those who are farthest from grace, in order to rediscover "the joy of God's tenderness." Let us pause for a moment and ponder the inspired words of the Bull of Indiction for the Extraordinary Jubilee of Mercy:

My thoughts now turn to the Mother of Mercy. May the sweetness of her countenance watch over us in this Holy Year, so that all of us may rediscover the joy of God's tenderness. No one has penetrated the profound mystery of the incarnation like Mary. Her entire life was patterned after the presence of mercy made flesh. The Mother of the Crucified and Risen One has entered the sanctuary of divine mercy because she participated intimately in the mystery of his love.

Chosen to be the Mother of the Son of God, Mary, from the outset, was prepared by the love of God to be the Ark of the Covenant between God and man. She treasured divine mercy in her heart in perfect harmony with her Son Jesus. Her hymn of praise, sung at the threshold of the home of Elizabeth, was dedicated to the mercy of God, which extends from "generation to generation" (Lk 1:50). We too were included in those prophetic words of the Virgin Mary. This will be a source of comfort and strength to us as we cross the threshold of the Holy Year to experience the fruits of divine mercy.

At the foot of the Cross, Mary, together with John, the disciple of love, witnessed the words of forgiveness spoken by Jesus. This supreme expression of mercy toward those who crucified him show us the point to which the mercy of God can reach. Mary attests that the mercy of the Son of God knows no bounds and extends to everyone, without exception. Let us address her in the words of the *Salve Regina*, a prayer ever ancient and ever new, so that she may never tire of turning her merciful eyes upon us and make us worthy to contemplate the face of mercy, her Son Jesus.[9]

This rich text reveals the intensity of the impassioned relationship that binds Pope Francis to Mary, Mother of Mercy. Let us pause for a prolonged, personal meditation on a few select passages:

"Her entire life was patterned after the presence of mercy made flesh."[10] Mary was chosen to be the mother

---

9. Pope Francis, Bull of Indiction for the Extraordinary Jubilee *Misericordiae Vultus*, April 11, 2015, no. 24, http://w2.vatican.va/content/francesco/en/bulls/documents/papa-francesco_bolla_20150411_misericordiae-vultus.html.

10. Francis, *Misericordiae Vultus*, no. 24.

of Jesus, sent by the Father to give us the gift of salvation. Blessed Alberione, echoing this, writes: "Bringing mercy to men and women is the reason for the incarnation."[11] Every particle of Mary's person was shaped by the presence of the Son, the incarnate mercy of the Father.

"Mary attests that the mercy of the Son of God knows no bounds"[12] and she does this above all at the foot of Jesus' cross, where she could hear words of forgiveness for his crucifiers. Mary, assuring us that no one is excluded from mercy, conquers all forms of distrust or fear. The mother who remains standing at the foot of the cross never grows tired of turning her eyes of mercy toward us. This is what moves us toward full confidence and encourages us to pray to Mary every day with that ancient yet ever new prayer, the *Salve Regina*. In this way, we become able to contemplate Jesus himself, the face of the Father's mercy.

---

11. James Alberione, *Donec formetus Christus in vobis* [Until Christ is formed in you], 3rd ed. (Cinisello Balsamo, Italy: San Paolo, 2008), 267.

12. Francis, *Misericordiae Vultus*, no. 24.

MAY

Mary in the Cenacle

The Month of Mary

All the faithful, especially those more devoted to Marian spirituality, welcome the month of May with joyful hearts. Popular piety has always linked the month of May to Mary. There is usually an upsurge of homilies, rituals, prayers, or Marian practices and praises that demonstrate the universality of love for and confidence in the Mother of God.

"Popular piety" is not equivalent to emotional or sentimental devotion, much less devotionalism. In *Evangelii Gaudium*, Pope Francis attempts to clarify the matter:

Popular piety enables us to see how the faith, once received, becomes embodied in a culture and is constantly passed on. Once looked down upon, popular piety came to be appreciated once more in the decades following the Council. In the Exhortation *Evangelii Nuntiandi*, Pope Paul VI gave a decisive impulse in this area. There he stated that popular piety "manifests a thirst for God which only the poor and the simple can know" and that "it makes people capable of generosity and sacrifice even to the point of heroism, when it is a question of bearing witness to belief."[1]

Well-known expressions of Marian spirituality are entirely justified, and all the more so if they are in "accord with the sacred liturgy."[2]

The month of May begins by celebrating Saint Joseph the Worker. At first it might seem that this feast is out of place, but it is not difficult to see the connection of this liturgical event to Marian spirituality. Joseph, a man of silence and work, of recollection and trust, loved *doing* more than speaking. How can we think of Joseph laboring at his workbench without seeing Mary alongside him?

Blessed Alberione points out this dynamic in the following words: "It was not a kind of work that drew the

---

1. Francis, *Evangelii Gaudium*, no. 123, citing from Pope Paul VI, Apostolic Exhortation *Evangelii nuntiandi*, no. 48, in *Acta Apostolica Sedis* 68 (1976), 38.

2. *Catechism of the Catholic Church: Second Edition. Revised in accordance with the official Latin text promulgated by Pope John Paul II* (Vatican City: Libreria Editrice Vaticana–United States Catholic Conference, Inc., 1997), no. 1675.

admiration of others, but the angels of heaven admired how it was carried out with perfect love of God, with all of the dignity and diligence of one who knows how to devote all things to the service of God."[3]

Mary in the Cenacle

In addition to the various Marian celebrations, the solemnity of Pentecost often falls in the month of May. The Acts of the Apostles recounts the descent of the Holy Spirit on the apostles, who were united and persevering in prayer:

> When they had entered the city, they went to the room upstairs where they were staying, Peter, and John, and James, and Andrew, Philip and Thomas, Bartholomew and Matthew, James son of Alphaeus, and Simon the Zealot, and Judas son of James. All these were constantly devoting themselves to prayer, together with certain women, including Mary the mother of Jesus, as well as his brothers. . . . When the day of Pentecost had come, they were all together in one place. And suddenly from heaven there came a sound like the rush of a violent wind, and it filled the entire house where they were sitting. Divided tongues, as of fire, appeared among them, and a tongue rested on each of them. All of them

---

3. Alberione, *Brevi meditazioni*, 379.

were filled with the Holy Spirit and began to speak in
other languages, as the Spirit gave them ability. (Acts
1:13–14; 2:1–4)

It is not possible to dissociate the Holy Spirit from
Mary: it is she who prepares souls to receive the Spirit
and the Spirit always has a preference for Mary's presence.
Saint Louis-Marie Grignion de Montfort was quite
convinced of this:

> God the Holy Spirit being barren in God—that is to
> say, not producing another Divine Person—is become
> fruitful by Mary, whom he has espoused. It is with her,
> in her, and of her, that he has produced his master-
> piece, which is God made man, and whom he goes on
> producing in the persons of his members daily to the
> end of the world. The predestined are the members of
> the Adorable Head. This is the reason why the more
> the Holy Spirit finds Mary, his dear and inseparable
> spouse,[4] in any soul, the more active and mighty he
> becomes in producing Jesus Christ in that soul, and
> that soul in Jesus Christ.[5]

In Mary who invokes and receives the Holy Spirit
in the Cenacle, Blessed Alberione sees the moment
emerge for her role as mother, teacher, and queen of the

---

4. The Second Vatican Council preferred to call Mary the "temple of the
Holy Spirit," rather than the spouse of the Holy Spirit, in order to avoid
confusion. See Second Vatican Council, *Lumen gentium*, no. 53.

5. De Montfort, *True Devotion*, 10–11.

apostles. He wrote and preached extensively on the title of Mary as Queen of the Apostles, proposing her to the Pauline Family as the Marian "devotion" par excellence, explaining in detail all the reasons for this in the third volume of *Maria Nostra Speranza*:

> Mary began her mission as Queen of the Apostles in the Cenacle. She gathered the apostles, comforted them, and supported them in prayer; she hoped, desired, and prayed with them. Her prayers were heard, and she received the Holy Spirit on the day of Pentecost with them.... Mary is the mother, teacher, and queen of the apostles because she has given us Jesus, fulfilling in this way the greatest apostolate: indeed, eternal salvation and all good things have come to us through Jesus Christ. Mary is the mother, teacher, and queen of the apostles because she exercised all the apostolates to the highest degree. There are various forms of apostolate in the Church: prayer, example, deeds, and word. Mary exercised all of them perfectly. Mary is also mother, teacher, and queen of the apostles because she possessed the gifts of an apostle to an eminent degree. She was chosen, the apostles recognized her as such, and she was crowned queen by the Most Holy Trinity. After the ascension of Jesus into heaven, Mary did not abandon the apostles even for a single moment: she followed them to the Upper Room, where she awaited the descent of the Holy Spirit with them. As an affectionate mother, authoritative teacher, and revered queen, she

sustained them, taught them, and protected them at all times. With what love she would have spoken to them about Jesus, recounting the events and episodes of her divine son's childhood and adolescence.[6]

Blessed Alberione's reflection on the Queen of the Apostles does not end here. For him, the Blessed Virgin manifested herself as Queen of the Apostles especially after her assumption into heaven. From that moment on, she has raised up every kind of apostle: of deeds and word, of example and pen, of charity and truth. Mary received from God the highest mission of calling and preparing apostles for all times and for every mission. And it is very consoling to think that Mary wants, close to her in heaven, all those who devote their energies to the apostolate, to make Jesus known and to give him to the world. May none of us miss this appointment!

Mary, Teacher of Prayer

In his encyclical *Dominum et Vivificantem*, Saint John Paul II sketches an image of Mary in relation to the Holy Spirit as follows:

In the midst of the problems, disappointments and hopes, desertions and returns of these times of ours,

---

6. James Alberione, "Feste di Maria," in *Maria nostra speranza* [Mary our hope], vol. III (Rome: Edizioni Paoline, 1955), 66–67.

the Church remains *faithful to the mystery of her birth.*
While it is an historical fact that the Church came
forth from the Upper Room on the day of Pentecost,
in a certain sense one can say that she has never left
it. Spiritually the event of Pentecost does not belong
only to the past: the Church is always in the Upper
Room that she bears in her heart. The Church perseveres *in prayer*, like the apostles *together with
Mary,* the Mother of Christ, and with those who in
Jerusalem were the first seed of the Christian community and who awaited in prayer the coming of the
Holy Spirit.

The Church perseveres in prayer with Mary. This
union of the praying Church with the Mother of
Christ has been part of the mystery of the Church
from the beginning: we see her present in this mystery as she is present in the mystery of her Son. It is the
Council that says to us: "*The Blessed Virgin* . . . over-
shadowed by the Holy Spirit . . . brought forth . . . the
Son . . . , he whom God placed as the first-born among
many brethren (see Rom 8:29), namely the faithful.
In their birth and development, she cooperates with a
maternal love"; she is through "his singular graces and
offices . . . intimately united with the Church . . . [She]
is a model of the Church" (Second Vatican Council,
Lumen Gentium, no. 63). "The Church, moreover,
contemplating Mary's mysterious sanctity, imitating
her charity, . . . *becomes herself a mother*" and "herself
is a virgin, who keeps . . . the fidelity she has pledged

to her Spouse. Imitating the Mother of the Lord, and by the power of the Holy Spirit, she preserves with virginal purity an integral faith, a firm hope, and a sincere charity." (Ibid., no. 64)[7]

This profound and engaging passage highlights two fundamental ecclesial characteristics:

a) *the Church "remains faithful to the mystery of her birth"*: since leaving the Upper Room on the day of Pentecost she has never departed from it; she lives in the Upper Room, the place she always "bears in her heart"[8];

b) *the Church perseveres in prayer*, as the apostles did with Mary, the Mother of Christ.

Mary emerges here as a true teacher of prayer: her care transforms men—who moments earlier were arguing among themselves about who was the greatest—into apostles "persevering with one mind in prayer."[9]

Saint Louis-Marie Grignion de Montfort comments as follows:

When we read, then, in the writings of Saints Bernard, Bernardine, Bonaventure, and others, that in heaven

---

7. John Paul II, Encyclical Letter *Dominum et Vivificantem*, May 18, 1986, no. 66, http://w2.vatican.va/content/john-paul-ii/en/encyclicals/documents/hf_jp-ii_enc_18051986_dominum-et-vivificantem.html.

8. Ibid.

9. Second Vatican Council, *Lumen Gentium*, no. 59, referencing Acts 1:14.

and on earth everything, even God himself, is subject
to the Blessed Virgin, they mean to say that the authority which God has been well pleased to give her is
so great, that it seems as if she has the same power as
God, and that her prayers and petitions are so powerful
with God, that they are likened to commands before
His Majesty, who never resists the prayer of his dear
Mother, because she is always humble and conformed
to his will.[10]

Mary cooperates with maternal love in the regeneration
and upbringing of her children, all of whom are destined
for redemption:

> The feast of Easter is the feast of redemption. . . . But
> the feast of Pentecost is the application of the redemp-
> tion. Redemption was accomplished on Calvary, but
> it has to reach souls. Otherwise, what good would
> it do? Hence Pentecost. When the apostles received
> the Holy Spirit, "*repleti sunt omnes Spiritu Sancto et
> coeperunt loqui*," they began to preach (see Acts 2:4),
> to share what they had heard from Jesus, what they had
> seen in Jesus, and what Jesus had demonstrated with
> his miracles, especially the resurrection.[11]

---

10. De Montfort, *True Devotion*, 14.

11. James Alberione, *Spiegazioni delle costituzioni 1961* [Explanation of
the constitutions, 1961] (Rome: Figlie di San Paolo, 2003), 215.

Our Lady of Fatima

The anniversary of the Virgin Mary's first apparition at Fatima is May 13. Faithful to her style, Mary chose three young shepherds, simple children intent on tending their flock, who already knew how to pray the rosary, just like Bernadette of Lourdes. We can see the preferences of God and Mary in this choice. Our Lady recommends the rosary to these little seers:

> Recite the rosary every day. Pray it to end the war, because only the Virgin can obtain this grace for humankind. Make sacrifices for sinners, and say this prayer often, but especially when making a sacrifice: "O Jesus, this is for love of you and for the conversion of sinners, and in reparation for the offenses committed against the Immaculate Heart of Mary."[12]

We can all confirm the power of Our Lady's intercession on May 13, 1981, when John Paul II fell victim to an attempt on his life at the hands of Mehmet Ali Ağca. The Pope was convinced that the hand of our Lady had deflected the bullet. He credited Mary with saving his life and wanted the bullet to remain forever set in the crown of the statue of the Virgin of Fatima.

---

12. James Alberione, *La Madonna di Fatima: Preghiamo il Cuore Immacolato di Maria* [Our Lady of Fatima: Let us pray to the Immaculate Heart of Mary] (Alba, Italy: Società Apostolato Stampa, 1942), 17–18.

The Feast of the Visitation

On May 31, the feast of the Visitation of the Blessed Virgin Mary to Saint Elizabeth closes the month dedicated to Mary. The Gospel tells us that Mary "set out and went with haste" to visit her cousin. On that occasion, it was the Spirit who proclaimed, "with a loud cry," through Elizabeth's mouth, that Mary was "blessed . . . among women" precisely because the fruit of her womb was blessed (see Lk 1:41–42). In her journey to her dear relative, Mary becomes the model of attentiveness and kindness. On this point, Blessed Alberione offers the following commentary:

> The most Blessed Virgin carried out a beautiful work of charity for her relative: she went quickly, she brought many blessings to that house, and she stayed there to offer humble and affectionate service. There she raised to God the hymn of humility and thankfulness: the *Magnificat*. In Mary, charity reaches the highest degree. She was destined to bring Jesus to men and women: this is her great gift . . . No greater gift can be given to others than Jesus.[13]

With Mary and like Mary, this is the invitation each one of us receives: to be and to become a gift to others, starting with those closest to us—all the time!

---

13. Alberione, *Brevi meditazioni*, 367.

JUNE

The Immaculate Heart of Mary

A Heart that Loves Us

From a liturgical perspective June is undoubtedly one of the most celebrated months of the year because we encounter a cascade of very important feasts: the Most Holy Trinity, the Most Holy Body and Blood of Christ, and the Most Sacred Heart of Jesus, which is linked to the memorial of the Immaculate Heart of Mary. The fact that the series of celebrations concludes with the diptych of the hearts of Jesus and Mary suggests that everything is born from and explained by divine love, which is always unconditional and surprising!

The liturgical celebration of the Heart of Mary, promoted by Saint John Eudes in the early 1600s, was extended to the universal Church in 1944 under the title of the Immaculate Heart of Mary. This was due especially to the influence of the apparitions at Fatima and the consecration of the whole human race to the Immaculate Heart of Mary by Pius XII before World War II:

> Queen of the Most Holy Rosary, Help of Christians, Refuge of Humanity, victor of all God's battles! In supplication we prostrate ourselves before your throne, confident to implore your mercy and receive the graces and necessary help and defense amid the present calamities, not by our own merits, but only through the immense goodness of your maternal heart.
>
> In this tragic hour of human history, we entrust and consecrate ourselves to your Immaculate Heart, not only in union with the Holy Church, the mystical body of your Jesus, who suffers and bleeds in so many places and is afflicted in so many ways, but also together with the whole world torn apart by violent conflicts.[1]

This feast was initially celebrated on August 22, within the octave of the Assumption. But now we celebrate the

---

1. Pius XII, Radiomessaggio: Preghiera per la consacrazione della Chiesa e del genere umano al Cuore Immacolato di Maria (Radio Message to Portugal: Prayer for the Consecration of the Church and the Whole Human Race to the Immaculate Heart of Mary), October 31, 1942, https://w2.vatican.va/content/pius-xii/it/speeches/1942/documents/hf_p-xii_spe_19421031_immaculata.html (translation John A. Di Camillo).

feast of the Immaculate Heart of Mary the day after the Solemnity of the Most Sacred Heart of Jesus, which seems more appropriate.

Mary and Jesus remain united always: in life, in heaven, and in worship. Mary continues to have the same thoughtful attention for each of us that she had for Jesus when he walked the streets of Galilee and Judea. Meditating at length on Mary and her love for us, Blessed Alberione writes:

> What are the qualities of this Heart? There are many. It is the Immaculate Heart; from the moment it was formed it was possessed by God; the devil could never even attempt to approach it. It is the most humble Heart; the words "Here am I, the servant of the Lord" (Lk 1:38) came from her Heart; so, the humble life of this most holy Virgin was always the expression of the sentiments of this Heart. It is a most pure Heart; it loved the Lord and only the Lord; and in the Lord it loved Saint Joseph, sinners, the hopeless, and the people of the world in which it lived. Mary died in an outpouring of perfect love for her God; and in heaven she lives of the love of God and love for all his children. It is a generous Heart; it was disposed to all God's wishes; even when it was a matter of difficult things; even during the passion and agony of the Son on the Cross.[2]

---

2. Alberione, *Brevi meditazioni*, 406.

Father Alberione wrote these reflections in 1948, a uniquely historical moment that reflected both the influence of Fatima and the horror of war. Everyone felt motivated to obtain the conversion of humanity through a singular commitment to avoid sin and remain faithful to God. Alberione loved to repeat that Mary knows how to look into our hearts with love and find its movements toward God: if it seeks God, if it is united to God, if it avoids everything that could displease God. In the various apparitions of our Lady, a recurrent theme was the desire to find in men and women dispositions of repentance to obtain God's forgiveness. Just think of the messages communicated to the visionaries of La Salette (1846), when Mary, with intense suffering, showed herself to be very worried about the fate of humanity: "If the people do not submit, I shall be forced to let fall the arm of my Son. It is so strong, so heavy that I can no longer withhold it . . . How long a time do I suffer for you!"

The invitation to conversion that poured from Mary's heart at La Salette was repeated some years later at Lourdes and then at Fatima. Since her spoken plea was not enough, our Lady broke down in tears. What message could be more penetrating and eloquent? Think also of the miraculous weeping that occurred in Syracuse (Sicily) in 1953, when tears flowed from a plaster sculpture of the Immaculate Heart of Mary. In that case, Mary did not utter a word—what a moving message! A year later, at the Sicilian regional Marian conference, on October 17, 1954, Pius XII sent a radio message to the world: "Will people understand the hidden language of those tears? O, the tears of Mary!"[3] The event in Syracuse does not seem to have been the only one. There are others not officially recognized by the Church. This assures us that in heaven there is a heart that loves us very much! Do we know how to respond?

Testimony of the Saints

It is significant that Jesus himself invites us to give ourselves to the loving heart of his mother. This stands out clearly in revelations to men and women mystics. During the season of Advent, the Lord spoke to Saint Mechtilde, a Benedictine mystic who lived in the second half of the thirteenth century in Germany, with these words:

> Greet my Mother's virginal heart in the abundance of all those goods that made it supremely useful to people. First, hers was the purest heart . . . Second, the most humble, for she specially deserved to conceive by the Holy Spirit. Third, the most devout and desiring, for by her heart's desire she drew me to herself. Fourth, the

3. Pius XII, Radiomessaggio [Radio message], October 17, 1954 (translation John A. Di Camillo).

most fervent in love to God and neighbor. Fifth, the most loyal, for she diligently treasured the memory of everything I did in my infancy, childhood, and youth (see Lk 2:51). Sixth, the most patient in my passion, which pierced her heart above all others in perpetual remembrance. Seventh, the most faithful, for she wanted her only child to be sacrificed for the world's redemption. Eight, the most solicitous in prayer, for she constantly interceded for the newborn Church. Ninth, the most assiduous in contemplation, acquiring grace for mortals by her merits.[4]

Who better than Jesus himself could have described for us the qualities of the Immaculate Heart of Mary? This was well understood by Saint Louis-Marie Grignion de Montfort, who spoke to those devoted to Mary in this way:

Though you, predestined souls, understand me well enough, I will speak yet more openly. Entrust not the gold of your charity, the silver of your purity, the waters of your heavenly graces, nor the wines of your merits and virtues to a torn sack, a broken coffer, a tainted vessel, like yourselves; else you will be stripped by the robbers. . . . Pour into the bosom and the heart of Mary all your treasures, all your graces, all your

---

4. Mechtilde of Hackeborn, *The Book of Special Grace*, tr. Barbara Newman (New York: Paulist Press, 2017), pt. 1, sec. 1.2, pp. 40–41.

virtues. She is a spiritual vessel, she is a vessel of honor, she is a marvelous vessel of devotion: *vas spirituale, vas honorabile, vas insigne devotionis*.[5]

From the day God himself took up his abode with all his perfections in that vessel it became totally spiritual, and the abode of the most spiritual souls. It has become honorable, and the throne of honor for the greatest princes of eternity. It has become wonderful in devotion, and an illustrious dwelling for gentleness, grace, and virtue. It has become rich as a house of gold, strong as a tower of David, and pure as a tower of ivory.[6]

And the writings of Blessed Alberione present the same tone of confidence and the same emphases. He thinks of Mary's heart first as a "burning censor," from which the fragrant incense of prayer arises:

In the house of Nazareth God was honored. A continuous incense of prayer would rise to God from Mary's heart, as from a burning censor. Her *mental prayer* is mentioned twice in the holy Gospel (see Lk 2:19, 51). She meditated first on the holy books; then she added meditation on the words and examples of Jesus and Joseph. Her *vocal prayer* consisted in psalms or expressions taken from Scripture, as the Magnificat

---

5. *Author's note*: Some of the invocations of the Litany of Loreto are in italics.

6. De Montfort, *True Devotion*, pt. II, sec. I, pp. 124–125.

demonstrates. *Lived prayer*, since Mary's day was always filled with humble works, but very welcomed by God because of the love that inspired them.[7]

Blessed Alberione highlights the habitual meditative listening of Mary's heart:

> She loved to remain united to her God in her heart, and rather than speaking much, the Gospel notes twice (see Lk 2:19, 51) that Mary listened especially to the words she heard from Jesus or from others about him, and she meditated on them in her heart. This is how Mary was prepared for the outpouring of the Holy Spirit, how she was always ready to hear the word of God: because she knew how to preserve intimate contemplation.[8]

The Heart of a Mother

From the many resources on the topic of the Immaculate Heart of Mary, let us ponder the moving words of John Paul II in his first encyclical, *Redemptor Hominis*:

> We can say that the mystery of the redemption took shape beneath the heart of the Virgin of Nazareth when she pronounced her "fiat." From then on, under the special influence of the Holy Spirit, this heart, the heart of both a virgin and a mother, has always followed

---

7. Alberione, *Brevi meditazioni*, 378.

8. James Alberione, *Alle Figlie di San Paolo: Meditazioni e istruzioni 1940–45* [To the Daughters of Saint Paul: Meditations and Instructions 1940–45] (Rome: Casa Generalizia Figlie di San Paolo: 2000), 449.

the work of her Son and has gone out to all those whom Christ has embraced and continues to embrace with inexhaustible love. For that reason, her heart must also have the inexhaustibility of a mother. The special characteristic of the motherly love that the Mother of God inserts in the mystery of the Redemption and the life of the Church finds expression in its exceptional closeness to man and all that happens to him. It is in this that the mystery of the Mother consists. The Church, which looks to her with altogether special love and hope, wishes to make this mystery her own in an ever-deeper manner. For in this the Church also recognizes the way for her daily life, which is each person.

The Father's eternal love, which has been manifested in the history of mankind through the Son whom the Father gave, "that whoever believes in him should not perish but have eternal life" (Jn 3:16), comes close to each of us through this Mother and thus takes on tokens that are of more easy understanding and access by each person. Consequently, Mary must be on all the ways for the Church's daily life. Through her maternal presence the Church acquires certainty that she is truly living the life of her Master and Lord and that she is living the mystery of the Redemption in all its life-giving profundity and fullness.[9]

---

9. John Paul II, Encyclical Letter *Redemptoris Hominis*, March 4, 1979, no. 22, http://w2.vatican.va/content/john-paul-ii/en/encyclicals/documents/hf_jp-ii_enc_04031979_redemptor-hominis.html.

It seems opportune to pause and reflect for a moment on some of the meaningful phrases used by Saint John Paul II to describe the correlation between the event of the redemption and the heart of Mary.

The Pope affirms that first of all this mystery took shape "beneath the heart of the Virgin of Nazareth" in the moment she responded to the angel's proposal with her *fiat*. In this way, Mary instilled her virginal love into the mystery of redemption and into the life of the Church. From this it follows that "her heart must also have the inexhaustibility of a mother": Mary is always present wherever Jesus is working, and she turns her tender and compassionate gaze "to all those whom Christ has embraced and continues to embrace with inexhaustible love." This "motherly love" draws close to every person whatever their circumstances. Through Mary, "the Father's eternal love"—which already found its highest expression in sending his beloved Son for our salvation—"comes close to each of us" through comprehensible and accessible signs and forms.

O, marvelous manifestation of limitless love!

Each member of the Church is called to take Mary as a model and become a visible extension of her, precisely because "Mary must be on all the ways for the Church's daily life."

JULY

Our Lady of Mount Carmel

The Scapular Devotion

From a Marian perspective, the most significant celebration in the month of July falls on the sixteenth, with the memorial of Our Lady of Mount Carmel. Although the liturgy ranks it as an optional memorial, there is little doubt that the feast of Our Lady of Mount Carmel remains one of Christianity's most loved.

Marian scholars point out that this devotion originated at a time preceding Mary's birth. It dates back to the great prophet Elijah (ninth century B.C.), who lived for some time on Mount Carmel with a community of the faithful who defended the purity of faith in God, in opposition to the priests of Baal.

We read in the First Book of Kings that the prophet had a vision: "Look, a little cloud no bigger than a person's hand is rising out of the sea" (1 Kgs 18:44), bringing rain that saves Israel from a terrible drought. We know that in that little cloud, "no bigger than a person's hand," rising from the sea toward Mount Carmel, saints—and mystics—have glimpsed the Virgin Mary who carries the Word of God in her womb and, giving him to the world, obtains the waters of divine grace.

Saint Louis-Marie Grignion de Montfort sees in the little cloud not only Mary, but also the missionaries whom God would raise up for his Company of Mary: they will be "men similar to clouds raised up from the earth and filled with heavenly dew, ready to fly wherever the breath of the Holy Spirit moves them."[1] Following the example of the prophet Elijah who recovers his strength on the mountain of the covenant, the saint asks that his missionaries live on the holy mountain of Mary: a mountain with which God is thoroughly pleased.

It is known that the feast of Our Lady of Mount Carmel was set on July 16 because, according to tradition, that was the day Mary appeared to the Carmelite friar Saint Simon Stock:

> The year was 1245 and the Carmelite religious had gathered for a General Chapter in England to elect a

---

1. See Louis-Marie Grignion de Montfort, *Preghiera infuocata* [Ardent Prayer] (Rome: Centro Mariano Montfortano, 1963), translation John A. Di Camillo.

superior. Simon Stock was elected, well known because of his noble birth and outstanding virtues. Desiring to increase veneration and devotion to Mary, he constantly begged her to grant her followers a sign of her benevolence. Then one day while he was absorbed in fervent prayer, the heavenly queen, accompanied by the angels, appeared to him. She showed him the holy habit and said to him: "Take this scapular, my beloved child, with which I desire your Order to be adorned, and the visible sign under which I desire that, from this day forward, all who wish to be among the number of my privileged children and of your brothers should join. Through this scapular I am establishing an eternal alliance and peace between the people and me. And, so that they remain faithful to me, I promise them protection from dangers, health in this life, and endless glory in the next."[2]

Later, appearing to Pope John XXII, Our Lady instructed him to confirm this privilege. She added that those who would choose to keep the scapular always with them, while accepting the other conditions as well, would be freed from purgatory on the first Saturday after their death. Although not all scholars agree on the authenticity of this apparition of the Virgin to the Pope, or even on the related papal bull concerning the privilege of the

---

2. Alberione, "Le Feste di Maria Santissima," in *Maria nostra speranza*, vol. II, 146.

scapular, the fact remains that many people of every age and social status honor Mary under the title of Our Lady of Mount Carmel.

In the same way, even kings and numerous popes wished to wear the scapular: Pius XII openly encouraged it, affirming that the devotion to the scapular had already poured out rivers of spiritual and temporal graces into the world. He was followed in this by Pope Roncalli, now Saint John XXIII.

Wearing the scapular certainly does not exhaust the devotion to Our Lady of Mount Carmel. On the contrary, it is a sign that invites us on a journey toward an ever more filial relationship with Mary. Blessed Alberione advises us to ask two graces of the Virgin of Carmel: the first is deliverance from eternal damnation, as well as deliverance from the pains of purgatory; the second is zeal for the salvation of souls.

> In the various circumstances of life, in her mission, in the practices of piety that she inspired, one thing predominates: she is the Co-Redemptrix; she is the Apostle, in the incarnation of the Word as on Calvary; at Pentecost, as in heaven; in inspiring the Rosary, as in the revelations of the scapular of Mount Carmel. Let us imitate her, let us give ourselves to the apostolate, let us save souls.[3]

---

3. Alberione, "Feste di Maria," 111.

Consecration to Mary

Devotion to Our Lady of Mount Carmel, also due to the use of the scapular, has powerfully penetrated the sensitivity of the Christian people. As Saint Paul VI indicated, it "can truly be considered ecclesial."[4] The Carmelite fathers, "brothers of the Blessed Virgin Mary of Mount Carmel," commenting on the sign of the scapular, reveal that wearing the scapular is a matter of an intentional choice motivated by faith and love. It is a decision that manifests consecration to Mary with a specific interior disposition to cultivate, namely, the sincere desire to imitate her. By this the faithful intend to penetrate the mystery of Mary's interior life, of her loving service and her constant union with Jesus Christ. It is a choice that extends to one's entire life, shapes our interior dispositions and relations with others, and inspires the will to do everything as Mary would have done it. Understood in this way, such a consecration is neither overly intimate nor excessively devotional: the emphasis is not on the number of devout practices, but on one's growth of faith in God to which Mary leads us. What is the Mother's greatest desire, but that her Son reign in our hearts?

---

4. Paul VI, Apostolic Exhortation *Marialis Cultus*, February 2, 1974, no. 8, http://w2.vatican.va/content/paul-vi/en/apost_exhortations/documents/hf_p-vi_exh_19740202_marialis-cultus.html.

The Church herself continues to propose to us the imitation of Mary, the first Christian[5] and the model of every person who wishes to live to the fullest a relationship of friendship and love with God.

The Collect for the celebration on July 16 urges us to invoke the Virgin's help in order to happily reach the holy mountain, which is Christ. Consecration to our Lady requires working for her honor. Her devotees, as affectionate children, seek to make her known and loved, through all the means at their disposal. It is therefore a devotion that enters into the fabric of Christian life as a reason for hope and a motivation for greater fidelity to God and the Church. Those who wear the scapular commit themselves to the service of Christ with the intention to live as brothers and sisters of Mary, in accord with Carmelite spirituality. An authentic devotion leads the faithful to open themselves to Mary, allowing her to enter more and more into their daily life. The most fervent desire would be to imitate the Blessed Virgin who treasured the word of God in her heart (see Lk 2:19, 51), to devote time to encounter God in prayer (liturgical prayer, praying the psalms, praying the Rosary), and to nurture the eucharistic life. In this way life gradually becomes prayer, even amid one's various commitments.

---

5. See J. Aldazabal, *Maria: la prima cristiana* [Mary: The First Christian] (Vatican City: Libreria Editrice Vaticana, 1995).

Blessed Alberione encouraged fostering devotion to Our Lady of Mount Carmel and, referring to one of the beliefs of his time, he affirmed: "Our Lady of Mount Carmel sometimes grants to those who wear her habit [scapular] and faithfully observe what is prescribed, a twofold mercy: she frees them as quickly as possible from the pains of purgatory or they avoid purgatory altogether."[6]

Although many today might be perplexed by this promise, Alberione's comment is beautiful and comforting: "Let us pray to Mary to free the souls in purgatory. If we pray for those souls, we will secure heaven for ourselves, because we will find as much mercy as we have shown toward others."[7]

Mary, Temple of Silence

Christian tradition, and especially Marian tradition, has always related the Virgin of Mount Carmel to the contemplative dimension of life. Benedict XVI often defined Our Lady of Mount Carmel as "a model of prayer, contemplation, and dedication to God."[8] During this

---

6. Alberione, *Maria nostra speranza*, 147.

7. Ibid., 149.

8. Benedict XVI, Angelus, July 16, 2006, https://w2.vatican.va/content/benedict-xvi/en/angelus/2006/documents/hf_ben-xvi_ang_20060716.html.

month of July, therefore, we want to welcome Mary's invitation to introduce us into a climate of prayerful silence that leads to contemplation. We must allow ourselves to become immersed in God, giving him our whole person. Saint Paul VI defined contemplation as the act that can offer a hierarchy for the immense pyramid of human activities:

> God is—and more, he is real, he lives, a personal, provident God, infinitely good; and not only good in himself, but also immeasurably good to us. He will be recognized as our Creator, our truth, our happiness; so much so that the effort to look on him, and to center our heart in him which we call contemplation, is the highest, the most perfect act of the spirit, the act which even today can and must be at the apex of all human activity.[9]

It is impressive how relevant to the present times this is! *Contemplate* (the letter of the Congregation for the Institutes of Consecrated Life and Apostolic Societies), speaks to the value of contemplation as the fullest act of the spirit. The letter contains timely reflections that are meaningful for every believer. The present culture,

---

9. Paul VI, Address during the Last General Meeting of the Second Vatican Council, December 7, 1965, http://w2.vatican.va/content/paul-vi/en/speeches/1965/documents/hf_p-vi_spe_19651207_epilogo-concilio.html.

especially Western culture, seems to be increasingly directed toward praxis: everything is aimed at doing and producing. This generates a countereffect—the unconscious need for silence, listening, and contemplative relief. The admirable icon of the contemplative attitude always remains the Virgin Mary, who is seen in this document as "the enchanted bride who adores."

Woman Clothed with the Sun

Our thoughts turn to Mary, the ark of God. Alongside her child, flesh of her flesh and whose origin is from on high, Mary is united to the Mystery. Profound happiness and endless paradox. She becomes the temple of silence without which the seed of the Word does not take root and reverence for God and his wonders does not flourish; the place in which the resonance of the Word and the voice of the Spirit are felt, like a gentle breeze. Mary becomes the enchanted bride who adores.

The divine event wondrously accomplished in her is welcomed into the bridal chamber of her life: *Adorna thalamum tuum, Sion, / Virgo post partum, quem genuit adoravit* ("Zion, let your wedding chamber be prepared ... / The Virgin conceived and gave birth to a son, / ... She knelt in worship before her child"[10]).

---

10. *The Office of Readings,* Responsory for the Feast of the Presentation of the Lord.

Mary becomes the treasure chest for mementos of the child, deeds and words compared with the foretelling of the prophets (see Lk 2:19), pondered with the Scriptures in the depths of her heart. She jealously keeps all those things she is unable to understand, awaiting the revelation of the mystery (*Contemplate*, no. 74).

We are therefore invited to fix our eyes on Mary, the "temple of silence," who welcomes the divine event "in the bridal chamber of her life." She is the same prayerful Virgin who enables us to translate the contemplative moment into a concrete commitment of apostolic dedication.

In his encyclical letter *Redemptoris Missio*, John Paul II affirms that a missionary is a "contemplative in action" and every believer must be a missionary in the environment in which he or she lives and works. "Unless the missionary is a contemplative, he cannot proclaim Christ in a credible way," and "he finds answers to problems in the light of God's word and in personal and community prayer."[11] Each of us is called to become a witness to the experience of God, and to affirm together with the apostles: "What we have heard, what we have seen with our eyes, what we have looked at and touched with our hands, concerning the word of life ... we declare to you" (1 Jn 1:1, 3).

---

11. John Paul II, Encyclical Letter *Redemptoris Missio*, December 7, 1990, no. 91, http://w2.vatican.va/content/john-paul-ii/en/encyclicals/documents/hf_jp-ii_enc_07121990_redemptoris-missio.html.

AUGUST

The Assumption and Queenship of the Blessed Virgin Mary

Our Heavenly Mother Awaits Us

For many people, the word "August" suggests vacations, beaches, mountains, holidays, resorts, travels away from home, and so forth. After a year of hard work, to take some time for rest and peaceful relaxation is a legitimate and reasonable duty to ourselves. Unfortunately, some see it as a time for excess. And yet, if there is a month that calls to mind good thoughts for believers—heavenly thoughts—it is precisely August.

The Solemnity of the Assumption of Mary occurs on August 15, the heart of the month, and a week later we celebrate the memorial of Mary, Queen of Heaven and Earth. The liturgical renewal desired by the Council places the feast of the Queenship of Mary as a complement to the Assumption because they form a single mystery, which we contemplate in the fourth and fifth glorious mysteries of the rosary.

Thinking about the Assumption means reflecting on the mystery of life in its totality. At the same time, it reminds us that we have a mother in heaven who is powerful in love, who awaits us, and who takes care of us. For this reason, the Assumption of the Blessed Virgin is a feast dear to our hearts because Mary was crowned queen in order to reach out to help her children. Mary is rich with the riches of heaven, which are destined for us as well.

Just as she is so full of grace as to pour it out onto all men and women, she is likewise so filled with glory as to use her power, her wisdom, and her love for our benefit. Contemplating Mary's Assumption into heaven inspired this prayer to flow from the heart of Blessed Alberione:

> O Mother, you are in the presence of the Trinity, speak well of us, that is, speak of our needs; pardon our weaknesses before the Trinity and obtain for us God's mercy. You know how many things are necessary for us: heavenly knowledge, fortitude to live according to the religious virtues; at the same time, we need humility and confidence. We need you to form our hearts as you formed the heart of the Immaculate Lamb, Jesus, your son. It is from your blood that the Most Sacred Heart

of Jesus was formed. So too form our hearts, that they may be generous, pious, and strong, and that they may be wholly enflamed with two loves: love God and love of neighbor.[1]

Just as he fixed his gaze on this mother, Blessed Alberione urged us to never allow ourselves to become discouraged: "Let no one be discouraged, because there is a mother above, in the house of our Father, who speaks of us and on our behalf."[2] Saint Louis-Marie Grignion de Montfort lived in the same Marian environment. According to him, to meditate on Mary assumed into heaven requires being open to God, capable of overcoming evil, and destined to be fully with God.

Mary, Queen of Heaven

As already mentioned, August brings another celebration: the memorial of the Queenship of the Blessed Virgin Mary, which is celebrated on August 22, seven days after the Solemnity of the Assumption. For a whole week we are invited to turn our gaze toward heaven, to contemplate Mary at the conclusion of her earthly life. Blessed Alberione rejoiced in meditating on these events! A hymn of joy burst forth from his heart at

---

1. Alberione, *Per un rinnovamento*, 167.
2. Ibid.

the thought that we have a powerful mother in heaven who takes care of us.

But he also urged us to examine our lives on "whether we fulfill well the four duties we have toward this good mother." He summarized them as follows:

Get to know her ever better. Do we read the best books about the Blessed Virgin? In our readings do we advance, according to our age and education? And on Saturdays do we try to meditate on Mary? Instruction should be the *first step* in devotion to Mary.

Second step: Imitate Mary. There was never a creature who loved the Lord with a more ardent love, and no apostle will ever love souls as much as Mary— through Jesus Christ—has loved and benefited them. Imitate her especially in the virtues of faith, hope, and charity.

Third step: Pray to Mary and trust in her. Do we pray to Mary? Consider whether we have confidence in this good mother, a confidence that touches her heart. Be simple children, aware of having an ever-greater need of this good mother's care.

Fourth step: Speak about Mary. Yes, our apostolate must aim for this: make Mary known and bring souls to Mary. Those who love their mother will speak often of her.[3]

---

3. Ibid., 167–69.

On August 22 we fix our gaze on Mary, crowned queen of heaven and earth. Mary is made queen to help her children and, according to most spiritual writers, she is in heaven to receive the reward she merited and to exercise her office of imparting graces, giving Jesus to souls. In fact, Saint Bernard comments as follows:

> Take away the sun that enlightens, warms, and makes all things fertile. What will remain on the earth except darkness, a deathly coldness that saddens nature? This is what would happen if the shower of graces that the Mother of God sends down were to cease. What would remain for us, then, but hardships, sorrow, and death?[4]

The Secret of Mary

The celebrations of the Assumption and the Queenship of Mary prove to be well-timed to confirm us in true devotion to the Mother of God. Once again, let us allow ourselves to be guided by the wise thoughts of Saint Louis-Marie Grignion de Montfort, who introduces a very persuasive image when speaking about Mary's role in salvation history:

> Now, a sculptor may craft a statue or natural like- ness in two ways: 1. out of some hard and shapeless

4. Alberione, *Brevi meditazioni*, 399.

material using his skill, strength, knowledge, and proper instruments; 2. he may cast it in a mold. The first method is long and difficult and is subject to many accidents: it could happen that an awkward blow of the hammer or chisel would spoil the whole work. The second manner is quick, easy, and gentle, with little effort or expense, provided the mold is perfect, and a good natural likeness, and the material used offers no resistance to the hand.

Mary most holy is the great mold of God, prepared by the Holy Spirit, to form a God-Man through the hypostatic union, and a Man-God through grace. In this mold, no feature of the Godhead is wanting; whoever is cast in it, and allows himself to be freely handled, receives all the features of Jesus Christ, who is True God. And this is done in a gentle manner, and in proportion to one's human weakness, without much pain or labor; in a sure manner, without fear of illusion, for the devil has never had, and never will have, access to Mary; and lastly, in a holy and spotless manner, without the shadow of the least stain of sin.[5]

What a gift to discover this secret along the first steps of a spiritual journey!

Happy, and a thousand times happy, is the soul here below to which the Holy Spirit reveals, and makes known,

---

the Secret of Mary; to which he opens this "garden enclosed," by permitting the soul to enter; to which he gives access to this "fountain sealed," by allowing the soul to drink deeply of the living waters of grace! Such a soul will find God alone in this most sweet creature, but God at the same time infinitely holy and exalted, infinitely condescending and proportioned to the soul's weakness. Since God is everywhere, he may be found everywhere, even in hell; but there is no place in which a creature can find him closer, and more proportioned to its weakness, than in Mary, for it was for this end that he came down into her bosom. Everywhere else he is the bread of the strong, the bread of angels, but in Mary he is the bread of children.[6]

So, is everything easy then, for the person devoted to Mary? Will there be no difficulties of any kind encountered along the way?

De Montfort is clear about this. There will be trials for everyone, but with Mary's help they will be "sweet" trials, enabling a person to bear them "with patience, and even with joy":

> Not that he who has found Mary, by true devotion, will be exempt from crosses, and sufferings: far from it, he is more assailed by them than any other, because Mary, being the mother of all the living, gives to her children

---

6. Ibid., 16–17.

pieces of the Tree of Life, which is the cross of Jesus; but in allotting these good crosses, she obtains the grace to carry them with patience, and even with joy, so that the crosses which she gives to those who belong to her are sweet rather than bitter crosses. Or, if for a while her children feel the bitterness of the chalice which they must drink in order to be the friends of God, the consolation and joy which this good mother gives after this sorrow, encourages them to carry still heavier and more bitter crosses.[7]

May we be always with Mary and like Mary!

---

7. Ibid., 18–19.

SEPTEMBER

The Nativity of the Blessed Virgin Mary

Under Mary's Protection

The passing of days quickly leads us to the feast of the Nativity of the Blessed Virgin Mary, celebrated by the Church on September 8. Behold the dawn that precedes the divine sun, Jesus Christ.

In communion with the mystics of all times, we welcome Mary, she who is truly pure, she who is the glory of Israel, she who is the joy of the world, she who is the hope of humanity. Mary appears immaculate and innocent: no light can compare with the radiance of her soul. For us, the month of September typically marks a return to all sorts of activities. How wonderful and promising that this takes place under Mary's protection.

She takes us by the hand with maternal care, fills us with confidence, and assures us of her continual assistance.

"*Ipsa duce non fatigaris*" (if she guides you, you will not tire) was the conviction of Saint Bernard of Clairvaux: under her guidance you will have no difficulty walking the paths that the Father's generosity opens before you each day!

Mary, Joy of the Trinity

In beginning the month of September, let us again allow ourselves to be enveloped in the contemplative attitude of Blessed Alberione. Humanity awaited and longed for this dawn, the messenger of the sun of justice, Christ Jesus. In the Immaculate Conception we have the dawn; in the birth of Christ, the daybreak.[1] It is moving how he loves to think of Mary as a cause of indescribable joy for the three Divine Persons:

> Mary, *joy of the Father*, who if pleased with creation, was much more pleased with Mary, the masterpiece of his hands; *joy of the Son*, who in Mary contemplated the tabernacle in which he would become flesh, the mother of whom he would be born; *joy of the Spirit*, who saw in her his most pure and faithful spouse, upon whom he would descend to form the Christ. And that is not

---

1. See Alberione, *Brevi meditazioni*, 359.

all: Mary is also the joy of the world and the joy of our soul, since she is the reason and the cause of our joy, wellbeing, and eternal happiness.[2]

Saint Louis-Marie Grignion de Montfort takes a different perspective. He prefers to meditate on Mary's desire to remain hidden even from the eyes of the angels:

He heard her prayers when she begged to be hidden, to be humbled, and to be treated as in all respects poor and of no account. He took pleasure in hiding her from all human creatures, in her conception, in her birth, in her life, and in her resurrection and assumption. Even her parents did not know her, and the angels often asked one another: *Quæ est ista?* "Who is that?" because the Most High either had hidden her from them, or if he did reveal anything, it was nothing compared to what he kept undisclosed.[3]

Mary, Star of the New Evangelization

The month of September, at least in the northern hemisphere, marks the return to social, community, and Church activities. How can we not think about the task of the new evangelization? How can we not recall the appeals of the recent popes?

---

2. See ibid., 359–60.
3. De Montfort, *True Devotion*, 1–2.

In his apostolic exhortation *Evangelii Gaudium*, Pope Francis proposed guidelines to encourage and guide a new phase of evangelization throughout the entire Church.[4] Proclamation is the first task of the Church, and the greatest challenge.[5] At the conclusion of the exhortation, the Pope asks Mary, "Mother of the living Gospel," to intercede so that this invitation "will be accepted by the entire ecclesial community."[6] May she help us to proclaim the message of salvation to all, raising up new disciples. "There is a Marian 'style' to the Church's work of evangelization. Whenever we look to Mary, we come to believe once again in the revolutionary nature of love and tenderness. . . . This interplay of justice and tenderness, of contemplation and concern for others, is what makes the ecclesial community look to Mary as a model of evangelization."[7]

Inviting all to move forward confidently toward Jesus' promise, "I am making all things new" (Rev 21:5), Pope Francis encourages us to turn to Mary with these words:

Mary, Virgin and Mother,
you who, moved by the Holy Spirit,
welcomed the word of life
in the depths of your humble faith:

---

4. See Francis, *Evangelii Gaudium*, no. 17.
5. See ibid., no. 15.
6. *Evangelii Gaudium*, no. 287.
7. Ibid., no. 288.

as you gave yourself completely to the Eternal One,
help us to say our own "yes"
to the urgent call, as pressing as ever,
to proclaim the good news of Jesus.

Filled with Christ's presence,
you brought joy to John the Baptist,
making him exult in the womb of his mother.
Brimming over with joy,
you sang of the great things done by God.
Standing at the foot of the cross
with unyielding faith,
you received the joyful comfort of the resurrection,
and joined the disciples in awaiting the Spirit
so that the evangelizing Church might be born.

Obtain for us now a new ardor born of the resurrection,
that we may bring to all the Gospel of life
which triumphs over death.
Give us a holy courage to seek new paths,
that the gift of unfading beauty
may reach every man and woman.

Virgin of listening and contemplation,
Mother of love, Bride of the eternal wedding feast,
pray for the Church, whose pure icon you are,
that she may never be closed in on herself
or lose her passion for establishing God's kingdom.

Star of the new evangelization,
help us to bear radiant witness to communion,
service, ardent and generous faith,

justice and love of the poor,
that the joy of the Gospel
may reach to the ends of the earth,
illuminating even the fringes of our world.

Mother of the living Gospel,
wellspring of happiness for God's little ones,
pray for us.

Amen. Alleluia![8]

The Pope asks Mary, virgin and mother, to help us say our "yes" amid the pressing urgency to make the Good News of Jesus resound, and to have the "holy courage" to identify "new paths" for the Gospel, defined as "the gift of unfading beauty." But the anthology of titles that Francis attributes to the Virgin is another moving example of his very affectionate relationship with the Mother of Jesus:

> "moved by the Holy Spirit";
>
> "gave yourself completely to the Eternal One";
>
> "filled with Christ's presence";
>
> "standing at the foot of the cross with unyielding faith";
>
> "Virgin of listening and contemplation";
>
> "mother of love";

---

8. Ibid., no. 288.

"bride of the eternal wedding feast";

"pure icon" of the Church;

"star of the new evangelization";

"Mother of the living Gospel"; and

"wellspring of happiness for God's little ones."

Mary is "a true mother, she walks at our side, she shares our struggles and she constantly surrounds us with God's love."[9]

---

9. Ibid., no. 286.

OCTOBER

Our Lady of the Rosary

A Prayer Based on the Gospel

In popular spirituality, the month of October is the month of the Rosary. The liturgical feast of Our Lady of the Rosary, celebrated October 7, is so deeply rooted in the hearts of the faithful that it guides our reflection for the entire month. There is no religious practice or "pious practice" that has received as much attention (especially from many popes) as has the Rosary.

In speaking to his priests, Blessed Alberione said: "In 1916, I wanted to count the number of encyclicals and articles that the popes had written about our Lady's Rosary. I counted about forty."[1]

---

1. A. Speciale, *Diario* [Diary], unpublished, February 23, 1952.

After Pius V, to whom we owe the traditional form of the Rosary, the pope most distinguished for his contributions to the topic was Leo XIII. This great pope wrote eleven encyclicals urging the faithful to the pious practice of praying the holy Rosary, especially during the month of October. And that is without counting his many other statements on the subject. Saint John XXIII listed Leo's encyclicals in his own encyclical *Grata Recordatio*[2] on praying the Rosary for the missions and for peace.

Pius XII defined the Rosary as "the compendium of the entire Gospel."[3] Paul VI, in his encyclical *Christi Matri* recalls how, in times of distress and uncertainty,[4] it is necessary to beg for peace through the intercession of the Virgin Mary.

And who does not remember how many times Saint John Paul II wrote and spoke on this topic, also wishing to personally participate in the communal prayer of the Rosary? The same can be said of Pope Benedict XVI.

---

2. See John XXIII, Encyclical Letter *Grata Recordatio*, September 26, 1959, no. 1, http://w2.vatican.va/content/john-xxiii/en/encyclicals/documents/hf_j-xxiii_enc_26091959_grata-recordatio.html.

3. Pius XII, Letter to the Archbishop of Manila "Philippinas Insulas," *Acta Apostolica Sedis* 38 (1946), 419, cited in Paul VI, Apostolic Exhortation *Marialis cultus*, February 2, 1974, no. 42, http://w2.vatican.va/content/paul-vi/en/apost_exhortations/documents/hf_p-vi_exh_19740202_marialis-cultus.html.

4. See Paul VI, Encyclical Letter *Christi Matri*, September 15, 1966, http://w2.vatican.va/content/paul-vi/en/encyclicals/documents/hf_p-vi_enc_15091966_christi-matri.html.

And Pope Francis? We all have the vivid memory of when he wished to publicly prescribe—as medicine for the soul—the "*misericordina*," a little box that looks like a medicine box but contains a rosary suitable for the chaplet of Divine Mercy. He distributed thousands of these during his Angelus message on November 17, 2013.

The Virgin Mary has shown in her apparitions that she is greatly pleased by this prayer of the Rosary, promising heavenly gifts to those who are faithful to it every day. Both at Lourdes and Fatima, Mary appeared with a rosary in her hands.

We know of course that there is resistance to this practice: not so much to the Rosary as a prayer, but rather to the way it is often recited as a mechanical repetition of formulas. For this very reason, the guidance given us by Paul VI in *Marialis Cultus* is particularly appropriate: he recommended the "renewal" of this prayer. The Pope highlighted the Rosary's fundamental characteristics, with their essential elements and mutual relationship.

> Thus, for instance, the Gospel inspiration of the Rosary has appeared more clearly: the Rosary draws from the Gospel the presentation of the mysteries and its main formulas. . . . The Rosary takes its inspiration from the Gospel to suggest the attitude with which the faithful should recite it. . . .
>
> The Rosary is therefore a prayer with a clearly Christological orientation. Its most characteristic

element, in fact, the litany-like succession of Hail Mary's, becomes in itself an unceasing praise of Christ. . . .

There has also been felt with greater urgency the need to point out once more the importance of a further essential element in the Rosary, in addition to the value of the elements of praise and petition, namely the element of contemplation. Without this the Rosary is a body without a soul . . . . By its nature the recitation of the Rosary calls for a quiet rhythm and a lingering pace, helping the individual to meditate on the mysteries of the Lord's life as seen through the eyes of her who was closest to the Lord. . . .

The Rosary is a practice of piety which easily harmonizes with the liturgy. . . . The commemoration in the liturgy and the contemplative remembrance proper to the Rosary . . . have as their object the same salvific events wrought by Christ.[5]

There is no doubt that if the Rosary is prayed as a living reading of the Gospel, a true encounter with Jesus, and a harmonious action of a greater liturgy, then the benefits Mary promised will be fulfilled: virtue and good works will flourish once again and will obtain God's generous blessings for souls.

---

5. Paul VI, *Marialis Cultus*, nos. 44, 46–48.

The Rosary of Blessed Alberione

Blessed Alberione says that praying the Rosary has three ends: to obtain Mary's mercy for today's society, for the Church, and for families; to reawaken faith through reflection on the principal mysteries of the Incarnation and life, passion, death, and resurrection of Jesus Christ; and to purify and elevate our spiritual life and assure our eternal salvation. Each mystery offers us a lesson to take away, a virtue to practice, and a grace to request. Little by little as we grow in devotion, we find different ways to meditate on the mysteries according to our own dispositions, inclinations, and needs. Referring to a text by the Dominican Jacques Marie Louis Monsabré, Father Alberione lists various themes for meditation on each mystery. These are his notes regarding Mary in the Rosary:

For the first joyful mystery we can meditate on the privileges of Mary. Her divine motherhood, her virginity, her sublime holiness, the Immaculate Conception, and her Assumption.

For the second joyful mystery: Mary as the universal mediatrix of grace. Whatever grace may be needed, we can always hope to obtain it through Mary.

For the third joyful mystery: Mary as Mother of God. Mother of God! This sweet title—Jesus pronounced it many times, when he called Mary his mother!

For the fourth joyful mystery: Mary as model of every virtue. Model of faith, hope, charity, purity, prudence, justice, fortitude, temperance, humility—model of every virtue.

For the fifth joyful mystery: the heart of Mary. Mary's heart is filled with love for God, filled with love for us; we can always turn to that heart.

For the first sorrowful mystery: Mary's life was a continual martyrdom. Saint Alphonsus explains that Mary's martyrdom was the longest because it lasted her entire life; the deepest, because it involved indescribable pains; the most meritorious, because Mary the Mother of Sorrows pleased her God.

For the second sorrowful mystery: the virginity of Mary. Blessed are the pure of heart, because they will please God and Mary. They will contemplate God in heaven and contemplate Mary.

For the third sorrowful mystery: the holiness of Mary. Mary's holiness surpasses that of all the saints and angels in heaven. She is a wonder of holiness.

For the fourth sorrowful mystery: Mary as Co-Redemptrix. Contemplate her on Calvary. Two altars: one is the altar of the Cross on which Jesus died and the other is Mary's heart, pierced by a sword of suffering.

For the fifth sorrowful mystery: Mary our Mother. Mary, the mother of Jesus and our mother. Our mother is so great, so powerful, so wise, with a heart that loves everyone.

For the first glorious mystery: Queen of heaven, rejoice! Congratulate Mary, because her son has conquered hell and death: he is risen. Let us ask for the grace that we, too, may rise again.

For the second glorious mystery: Mary's ascensions. Every day Mary made progress in holiness: ever greater faith, ever greater love, ever greater abandonment to God and to his will.

For the third glorious mystery: Mary as Queen of the Apostles. Mary among the apostles. We are all consecrated for the apostolate. And not a day goes by that we do not carry out some work ordered to the apostolate.

For the fourth glorious mystery: veneration of Mary. There is no nation in which the name of Mary is not honored and invoked. How many churches, feasts, images, and prayers to Mary!

For the fifth glorious mystery: the power of Mary. What God does by nature, Mary can do by her intercession with God. Close to God, she has an omnipotence of prayer.[6]

Which aspects of Mary would Father Alberione propose for meditation on the luminous mysteries? Let us make his certainty our own: if we recite the Rosary well, we will have the necessary graces for ourselves and for our apostolic work for our entire life. And when we have to take initiatives, or make some sacrifices, we will have our Mother with us.

---

6. Alberione, *Per un rinnovamento*, 263–67.

Do we understand what it means to have such a mother with us, to help us?

The Testimony of Pope Francis

On the occasion of the dedication of three mosaics at the shrine of Our Lady of Ta' Pinu in Gozo, Malta, Pope Francis said in a video message:

> The images in the parvis [churchyard] you are inaugurating today set before our eyes the beauty of a simple, contemplative prayer that is accessible to all, old and young: the prayer of the Holy Rosary. I also often recite the Rosary before a mosaic; a small mosaic of Our Lady and Child, in which it appears that Mary is at the center, whereas in reality, using her hands, she becomes a sort of ladder on which Jesus can descend among us. The center is always Jesus who humbles himself to walk among us men, so that we can ascend to heaven with him.
>
> In the prayer of the Rosary we turn to the Virgin Mary so that she may bring us ever closer to her son, Jesus, so as to know and love him more and more. And as we repeat "Hail Mary," we meditate on the mysteries, the joyous, luminous, painful, and glorious phases of Christ's life, but also of our lives because we journey with the Lord. This simple prayer, in fact, helps us to contemplate all that God in his love has done for us and for our salvation, and allows us to understand

that our life is united to Christ's. In prayer, we bring everything to God, our struggles, our wounds, our fears, but also our joys, our gifts, our loved ones . . . all to God. By praying, we allow God to enter our time, to welcome and transfigure all that we experience.

Often make use of this powerful instrument, the prayer of the Holy Rosary, because it brings peace to hearts, to families, the Church and the world.[7]

Even though Pope Francis maintains that the Rosary is a prayer accessible to everyone, others (for example, Hans Urs von Balthasar) say that it is a difficult prayer not held in high regard by everyone.[8] Perhaps this is because praying the Rosary requires contemplating the mysteries of the life of Jesus, as von Balthasar points out:

In the succession of Hail Marys, an endless realm in the world of prayer opens up before the contemplative, praying person: an expanse that he or she can travel in any direction without getting lost, because the reference point is Mary, in whom the mystery of the Trinity was revealed for the first time.[9]

---

7. Francis, Video Message to the Bishop of Gozo (Malta) on the Occasion of the Inauguration of the Mosaics of the Shrine Dedicated to Our Lady of Ta' Pinu, June 18, 2017, http://w2.vatican.va/content/francesco/en/messages/pont-messages/2017/documents/papa-francesco_20170618_videomessaggio-santuario-malta.html.

8. See Hans Urs von Balthasar, *Maria icona della Chiesa* [Mary, icon of the Church] (Cinisello Balsamo, Italy: San Paolo, 1998), 48.

9. Ibid. (translation John A. Di Camillo).

NOVEMBER

The Presentation of the Blessed Virgin Mary

The Protoevangelium of James

The month of November opens with two liturgical celebrations filled with light and hope: the Solemnity of All Saints and the Commemoration of All the Faithful Departed. It is a cause of profound joy to fix our gaze on the countless numbers of brothers and sisters who already enjoy the beatific vision of God.

From a Marian perspective, the most relevant celebration takes place on November 21: the memorial of the Presentation of the Blessed Virgin Mary in the Temple. This event in Mary's life precedes the angel's announcement. Little is known about this time; the canonical gospels do not mention it. The event is found only in an apocryphal gospel, the Protoevangelium of James. The writer offers rich details about the conception of Mary, her birth, her entering the Temple (to fulfill a vow made by her parents), and her marriage to Joseph. Particular attention is given to the moment when the little three-year-old Mary was taken to the Temple, where she would spend twelve long years in prayer, reflection, and spiritual formation.

The following is a descriptive excerpt from the Protoevangelium of James (7:2–3; 8:1):

> And when the child was three years old, Joachim said, "Summon the unsullied daughters of the Hebrews and let them take their lamps, and let them illuminate their lamps (while accompanying her) so that the child may not stray and her heart be captivated by other than the Temple of the Lord." And they did so until they came to the Temple of the Lord. And the priest received her, and lovingly praised her saying, "The Lord has blessed your name among all generations, and because of you the Lord will manifest his redemption of you till the end of days among the children of Israel."
>
> And he placed her on the third step of the altar, and the Lord placed grace upon her and she danced with her feet, and the whole house of Israel loved her.
>
> And her parents went back home marveling and praising almighty God, for she did not follow after them. And Mary was in the Temple of the Lord. She

was cared for like a dove and she received food from the hand of an angel.[1]

Recent scholarship has raised a number of questions about the historical authenticity of this account. Until a few decades ago, authors accepted its historicity without question, and this included Blessed Alberione. In the first edition (1939) of *Maria nostra speranza* (volume III: *Le Feste di Maria*), he called on the authority of Saint Evodius the martyr and Saint Germanus of Constantinople, and even cited the description by Saint Francis de Sales of Mary's journey to the Temple with her parents.

Aside from all this, it is the event's spiritual significance that matters: Mary consecrated herself totally in the first years of her life; the young girl was carefully prepared for the mission that the heavenly Father had reserved for her; and this preparation took place in an atmosphere of silence, recollection, and communion with God. Furthermore, the patristic and liturgical texts commenting on this event exalt Mary as the new and authentic temple of the Lord. God's presence in the ancient Temple of Israel finds in Mary an unheard-of yet very real fulfillment: in her virginal womb the Father forms the earthly dwelling of the Son! Mary then was not

---

1. Bertrand Buby, SM, tr., "Proto-Gospel of James" in *Mary of Galilee: The Marian Heritage of the Early Church,* vol. 3 (New York: Alba House, 1997), p. 41.

unprepared for such an event: the Spirit, who had already preserved her from any stain of sin, was forming her from a young age and to some extent was already predisposing her to follow the way Jesus would mark out.

The gift that Mary received from on high we try to attain through a daily response to our commitments. The goal is the same: to become a space open to the Spirit so as to live our consecration to the fullest, always aiming for union with our only head, Jesus.

> [Jesus Christ] is our only Master, who has to teach us; our only Lord, on whom we ought to depend; our only Head, to whom we must be united; our only Model to whom we should conform ourselves; our only Physician, who can heal us; our only Shepherd, who can feed us; our only Way, who can lead us; our only Truth, whom we must believe; our only Life, who can animate us; and our only All in all things, who can satisfy us.[2]

Pro Orantibus

Modeling their life on Mary, who gave herself completely to the Lord, countless individuals called by the unconditional love of the Father have followed the same path. Our thoughts go in particular to those called to the contemplative life. Because of his esteem for the

---

2. De Montfort, *True Devotion*, pt. I, sec. II, pp. 37–38.

contemplative life Pius XII instituted *Pro Orantibus* Day in 1953, to be celebrated on November 21, the liturgical feast of the Presentation of Mary in the Temple. The Latin phrase *pro Orantibus* means "for those who pray," and refers in a special way to all contemplative, cloistered vocations. Pope Francis noted:

> November 21 is the liturgical memorial of the Presentation of Mary Most Holy in the Temple, and we will celebrate the Day *pro Orantibus*, dedicated to the cloistered religious communities. It is an opportune occasion to thank the Lord for the gift of so many people who, in monasteries and hermitages, dedicate themselves to God in prayer and in silent work. Let us give thanks to the Lord for their witness of cloistered life and let us not fail to provide spiritual and material support to these, our brothers and sisters, so that they may fulfill their important mission.[3]

November 21 is a day that highlights the value of cloistered and contemplative vocations, and places appropriate emphasis on their unique importance. The lifestyle of persons called by God to a vocation, lived out in silence and continual prayer for the universal Church and for all peoples, reveals an incomparable wealth and

---

3. Francis, General Audience, November 20, 2013, http://w2.vatican.va/content/francesco/en/audiences/2013/documents/papa-francesco_20131120_udienza-generale.html.

richness—which for some is incomprehensible. As Louis-Marie Grignion de Montfort notes, for this way of life Mary's presence is irreplaceable.

> If devotion to the most holy Virgin Mary is necessary for all men and women simply for working out their salvation, it is still more so for those who are called to any particular perfection. I do not think anyone can acquire an intimate union with our Lord, and a perfect fidelity to the Holy Spirit, without a very great union with the most holy Virgin, and a great dependence on her assistance.[4]

Benedict XVI had already asked all the faithful to thank the Lord for their brothers and sisters who have embraced this mission of devoting themselves entirely to prayer and living on what they receive from Providence. And he continued: "Dear sisters and dear brothers, your presence in the Church and in the world is indispensable."[5] The difficult economic conditions that many monasteries experience, sometimes testing the limits of survival, are well known. For this reason, the Pope did not fail to add: "On our part let us pray for them and for new vocations and let us work to support monasteries in their material needs."[6]

---

4. De Montfort, *True Devotion*, pt. I, sec. I, pp. 23–24.

5. Benedict XVI, Angelus, November 16, 2008, http://w2.vatican.va/content/benedict-xvi/en/angelus/2008/documents/hf_ben-xvi_ang_20081116.html.

6. Ibid.

This is a specific duty of the Christian community, because supporting monasteries in their material needs means contributing to that part of the Church which, by its presence, continues to benefit the world.

O Mother, Help Our Faith!

In his encyclical *Lumen Fidei*, Pope Francis devotes the final chapter to the Virgin Mary as the one who preceded us, in an admirable way, on the pilgrimage of faith. The mention of a noble and good heart in the Gospel according to Luke (see Lk 8:15), which is a reference to the Word that has been heard and guarded, paints an implicit portrait of the Virgin Mary's faith. When our spiritual life bears fruit, we are filled with joy for the visible signs of a firm faith. All this spontaneously evokes a heartfelt prayer to Mary, mother of the Church and mother of our faith:

> Mother, help our faith!
> Open our ears to hear God's word
> and to recognize his voice and call.
> Awaken in us a desire to follow in his footsteps,
> to go forth from our own land and to receive
> his promise.
> Help us to be touched by his love,
> that we may touch him in faith.
> Help us to entrust ourselves fully to him

and to believe in his love, especially at times of trial,
beneath the shadow of the cross,
when our faith is called to mature.
Sow in our faith the joy of the Risen One.
Remind us that those who believe are never alone.
Teach us to see all things with the eyes of Jesus,
that he may be light for our path.
And may this light of faith always increase in us,
until the dawn of that undying day,
which is Christ himself, your Son, our Lord![7]

What matters most to Pope Francis is our faith. For this he prays to Mary, that she may "help"—which is to say strengthen, deepen, invigorate—the faith of believers. To that end, he lists the ways that faith can mature.

Open our ears to hear God's word. This is the first step. He asks our heavenly mother to open our minds and hearts to listen to the Word, who is Jesus. A profound listening will enable us to recognize the Lord's voice and respond with readiness.

Awaken in us a desire to follow in his footsteps. We ask Mary to awaken in us the desire to resolutely follow Jesus, day after day.

---

7. Francis, Encyclical Letter *Lumen Fidei*, June 29, 2013, no. 60, http://w2.vatican.va/content/francesco/en/encyclicals/documents/papa-francesco_20130629_enciclica-lumen-fidei.html.

Help us to be touched by his love. Jesus' love for humanity was given as a gift, and now is the time to allow ourselves to be touched by this love.

Help us to entrust ourselves fully to him. We are always in the realm of our response. We ask the Virgin to help us entrust ourselves, give ourselves, and totally abandon ourselves to Jesus.

Sow in our faith the joy of the Risen One. The meaning of a joyful faith becomes increasingly important. A gloomy faith would not be authentic!

Remind us that those who believe are never alone. If we believe, we do not run the risk of isolation. Faith places us in dialogue with Jesus and with all brothers and sisters who follow him.

Teach us to see all things with the eyes of Jesus. Only Mary can teach us how to evaluate people and situations through the eyes of Jesus. The eschatological perspective becomes ever brighter. The light of faith will grow in us until the day comes when the sun never sets, which is the same Christ, our Lord.

Imitate Mary

We are all familiar with the well-known work of Thomas à Kempis, *The Imitation of Christ.* Perhaps we are not as aware that he also penned another work: *The*

Imitation of Mary. In it, he invites us to have a most loving trust in the mother of Jesus:

> It is a good thing to always remember the glorious Virgin Mary, blessed Mother of the Lord Jesus, and entrust ourselves each day to her merits and prayers, having recourse to her for every need, as a wounded and shaken child runs back to his or her mother. Everyone therefore should call upon Mary, the righteous as well as sinners. Above all, religious men and women and those who are fervent in devotion should do so. They have made vows of chastity, and with pious longing have turned toward the things of heaven, unconcerned with earthly things.[8]

The author's attention seems to be directed primarily toward men and women in religious life, but the suggestions are also valid for "those who are fervent in devotion." He urges everyone to have complete trust in she who can grant the prayers of her devout children.

> What is fitting for you to ask of her? First of all the forgiveness of sins; then the virtue of chastity and the gift of humility, which is always pleasing to God, so that you will find yourself always humble before him and desire to be considered poor and lowly; lastly, ask that

---

8. Thomas à Kempis, *L'imitazione di Maria* [The Imitation of Mary] (Cinisello Balsamo, Italy: San Paolo, 2015), 29 (translation John A. Di Camillo).

you may never glory in anything, so that you do not lose everything you think you possess. Feel sorrow for the fact that you are so far from the real virtues, such as profound humility, holy poverty, perfect obedience, unsullied chastity, zealous prayer, and fervent charity. All of these virtues abide in the heart of Mary, the Mother of Jesus. Therefore, cast yourself at her feet like a beggar and plead to be able to obtain at least a small portion, since you cannot earn them fully because of your indifference.[9]

As indicated, the virtues to ask of Mary in order to better live out consecration to our Lord are quite specific. They are virtues that "abide in the heart of Mary": how could the Virgin deny them to those who ask with confidence?

Included is a recommendation to have contrition for the disparity between the ideal and our inadequate response. But believers have a powerful weapon: they entrust themselves to the very faithfulness of Mary, because her maternal prayers "are greatly welcomed by God" and always fulfilled:

Whatever your desires may be, pray with humility that they may be fulfilled through Mary's intercession. It is in fact by her glorious merits that all those who are in purgatory and on earth find assistance. Her grace

---

9. Ibid., 30 (translation John A. Di Camillo).

is immense, and immense is her glory in Jesus, who is her Savior and ours, greater than that of all the saints in heaven. But it all benefits us, who are on earth. Therefore, entrust yourself to her faithfulness, since her prayers are greatly welcomed by God and everything she asks and desires is pleasing to her and to her beloved Son, and beneficial for your salvation in accord with God's plan.[10]

---

10. Ibid. (translation John A. Di Camillo).

DECEMBER

Mary Immaculate

The Immaculate Conception

In the month of December, at the heart of Advent, we come upon the Solemnity of the Immaculate Conception.[1] The liturgy of the day invites us to praise God for the plan of salvation fully accomplished through Mary. It presents us with the well-known Protoevangelium of the Book of Genesis, in which the Fathers of the Church saw Jesus Christ and his mother prefigured:

> "I will put enmity between you and the woman,
> and between your offspring and hers;

---

1. The Immaculate Conception is a Catholic dogma (proclaimed by Pope Pius IX on December 8, 1854, with the bull *Ineffabilis Deus*) which declares that the Virgin Mary was preserved from original sin from the first moment of her conception and filled with grace.

he will strike your head,
    and you will strike his heel." (Gen 3:15)

Theological reflection on the Immaculate Conception emphasizes the resplendent sign of God's generous love; the perfect expression of the redemption accomplished by Christ; the fullness of innocence and holiness; and participation in divine life from the beginning, through preservation from the deadly influence of sin.

In this light, the Immaculate Conception is cause for complete confidence because the salvific power of God defeats evil and assures us that grace triumphs over sin. The Church has always recognized in the event of the Annunciation to Mary (see Lk 1:26–38) the fulfillment of the ancient and mysterious prophecy of Isaiah to King Ahaz: "Therefore the Lord himself will give you a sign. Look, the young woman is with child and shall bear a son, and shall name him Immanuel. He shall eat curds and honey by the time he knows how to refuse the evil and choose the good" (Is 7:14–15).

Emmanuel, God with us, is he who has already come in time and for whom we wait. He will return to us in the mystery of Christmas and will be a real person in the events of history: God among his people.

In contrast to the unbelief of King Ahaz is the faith of Mary, who confidently welcomes the great sign given to her, together with the other unique sign offered by the angel Gabriel in support of her faith journey: the extraordinary pregnancy of Elizabeth, who conceives a child in her old age (see Lk 1:36–37). Mary's faith becomes the good ground, blessed and full of grace, able to welcome the presence of the Lord; a vital space that allows God to enter into history and become fully involved in this adventure of ours, which appears so insignificant but is quite invaluable.

Through Mary's "yes" a new story begins: that of the God-with-us, prophesied by Isaiah. This story also becomes ours: the possibility of new life, a precious vessel in which to store the perfume of love, the fragrance of the gift of oneself.

Mary's faith opened up new spaces so God could create a new story within the uncertain and confused plot of events directed by humankind. Mary is blessed precisely because of her faith. "'Blessed is she who believed that there would be a fulfillment of what was spoken to her by the Lord.' . . . Surely, from now on all generations will call me blessed" (Lk 1:45, 48).

Nevertheless, the delights of faith in Mary's life are constantly marked by trials, darkness, and the cross. And yet she had heard the words of glory regarding the Son: "He will be great, and will be called the Son of the Most High, and the Lord God will give to him the throne of his ancestor David. He will reign over the house of Jacob forever, and of his kingdom there will be no end" (Lk 1:32–33).

The mystery of God had just become flesh in her when she was immediately left alone: "Then the angel departed from her" (Lk 1:38).

What must Mary have felt keeping this mystery to herself?

A divine mystery was entrusted to her, a girl from an unknown village in Galilee. What a trial it must have been for her to keep faith in the Son of the Most High, whose reign would never end (see Lk 1:32–33), while her son Jesus, in thirty years of hidden life, was considered to be only the humble son of a carpenter? Living so close to Jesus in the daily life of Nazareth characterizes the "mystery" of the life of Mary, whose profound acceptance occurred gradually through faith, to the point of heroism. John Paul II recalled and contemplated this journey in his encyclical *Redemptoris Mater*:

> And now, standing at the foot of the Cross, Mary is the witness, humanly speaking, of the complete negation of these words.[2] On that wood of the Cross her Son hangs in agony as one condemned. "He was despised and rejected by men; a man of sorrows . . . he was despised, and we esteemed him not": as one destroyed (see Is 53:3–5). How great, how heroic then is the obedience of faith shown by Mary.[3]

---

2. *Author's note*: This is a reference to the words of the angel Gabriel to Mary (see Lk 1:26–28).

3. John Paul II, *Redemptoris Mater*, no. 18.

The sign of Mary, but also the sign that is Mary, becomes the seal of faith in history. The great and solemn story blends continuously with the humble and simple one, the one made up of apparent failures and stained by visible inconsistencies, the one made up of fear and pain, the one steeped in silence or many questions. The entirety of this story, which is our story thanks to Mary's "yes," becomes the story of salvation, hope, and love.

Our Lady of Guadalupe

When Saint John Paul II visited the shrine of Our Lady of Guadalupe in 1999, he declared that her feast day (December 12) should be observed throughout the continent, for she is the patron of the Americas. Devotion to Mary under this title has been growing in recent years, as Our Lady of Guadalupe is taken as a patron by many in the pro-life movement. The lovely story of Mary's apparition to Saint Juan Diego is filled with expression of our heavenly mother's tender love.

Juan Diego was making his long trip to Mass on the cold morning of December 9, 1531, which at that time was the feast of the Immaculate Conception. Suddenly he heard some strains of beautiful music. Looking to see where it came from, Juan found himself at the top of Tepeyac Hill, near Mexico City. He was startled to see a beautiful young woman standing there. She looked like a morena, that is, one of his own people. In his own language, Nahuatl, she called him by name, using a nickname that showed great affection: "Juanito," she said, "Juan Dieguito, where are you going?"

Still stunned, Juan's words tumbled out, "I am on my way to Mass." The lady continued, "Know and understand, dearest of my children, that I am the ever-holy Virgin Mary, Mother of the true God who gives life, Mother of the Creator of heaven and earth."

The Virgin Mary told Juan that she wanted a church to be built on that spot. Why? Mary said that she wanted to "show forth all my love, compassion, assistance, and defense because I am your loving Mother: yours, and all who are with you, and of all who live in this land, and of all who love me, call to me, and trust in me. I will hear their cries and will give remedy to their sorrows and sufferings."

Then the beautiful Lady told Juan to bring her message to the bishop. Juan obeyed. But the bishop, Juan de Zumárraga, didn't believe that the Blessed Virgin Mary had really appeared to the humble man before him. Downhearted, Juan Diego left the bishop's residence. He again saw the Lady when he passed by Tepeyac and in dismay reported that he had failed. The Lady told him to go back and Juan Diego obeyed, but the bishop told him to ask for a sign. When Juan saw the lady again she consoled him and said, *"Do not let anything afflict you,*

*and do not be afraid of any illness, or accident, or pain.
Am I not here who am your Mother? Are you not under
my shadow and protection? Do you need anything else?"*

Then Mary told Juan to gather the flowers he would
find at the top of the hill and bring them to her. *Flowers
in December?* he wondered, but he obediently did as she
asked. He was amazed to find beautiful Castilian roses
at the peak of their bloom! He brought them to the
Lady, who lovingly arranged them in his tilma. He went
back to the bishop and when Juan opened his cloak the
beautiful roses spilled out. The bishop and others in the
room were astounded at what they saw: an image of the
Lady imprinted on Juan's tilma. This image, of course, is
the amazing icon of Our Lady of Guadalupe, patron of
Mexico and loving Mother of all people.

After she appeared to Juan Diego, many more
conversions occurred among the indigenous peoples.
Saint John Paul II had noted that Our Lady of Guadalupe
is the evangelizer of the Americas. Blessed Alberione
spoke about six ways in which Mary is an apostle:

> The first apostolate is a well-practiced interior life.
> The person who sanctifies himself is contributing to
> the whole Church, the mystical Body. For his part
> the holy person transfuses this body's circulation
> with a pure and immaculate blood. Because Mary
> is the holiest of creatures she contributed more
> than any others—apostles, martyrs, confessors,

virgins—to edify and make the Church beautiful and dynamic. The interior life is the soul of every apostolate.

Second apostolate: prayer. Saint James says: "Pray for one another, so that you may be healed. The prayer of the righteous is powerful and effective" (Jas 5:16). . . . Mary prayed more than all, better than all, for the needs of all.

Third apostolate: good example. "Let your light shine before others, so that they may see your good works and give glory to your Father in heaven" (Mt 5:16). . . . Good example is silent preaching, which starts from life and goes on reforming life. If words simply come out of your mouth they will only re-sound in a person's ears. Mary is our example in theo-logical, cardinal, and religious virtues.

Fourth apostolate: suffering. Jesus Christ re-deemed the world especially through his passion and death: "Through your holy cross and death you have redeemed the world." But there were two altars on Calvary: the cross of Jesus and the Heart of Mary. A spear pierced the Heart of Jesus; a sword pierced the soul of Mary. . . . All of us have so many sufferings to offer to the Lord in a spirit of apostolate.

Fifth apostolate: the word. Mary did not preach, but she certainly spoke with great charity and pru-dence at home and outside of it. Of her we have seven words that are true apostolate, the Magnificat being a special example. The Fathers tell us that it was Mary who revealed to Saint Luke the Gospel's infancy narratives. Even today every word of hers is light for contemplative souls.

Sixth apostolate: action. Mary's life before the Incarnation and during the thirty-three years passed with Jesus is an ongoing series of acts and deeds aimed at accomplishing her mission, her great apostolate. In the days following Jesus' Ascension, in the Cenacle, and during the period of early opposition and uncertainty when the Church was taking its first steps, it was Mary who consoled, comforted, and encouraged the Apostles.[4]

We can imitate Mary in leading others to Jesus. The six practical ways that Alberione outlines are things that each of us can do. No matter how small or seemingly insignificant, every prayer, suffering, action, and good word we can share with others plays its part in evangelizing the world.

The Christmas Season

An author who devoted many of his works to the mystery of the nativity was the poet and theologian Romanos the Melodist, born in Emesa (today Homs) in

---

4. Alberione, *Ut perfectus sit homo Dei* (Cinisello Balsamo, Milan: Edizioni San Paolo, 1998), 516–18.

Syria circa 490 A.D. In one of the *oikos*[5] of a Christmas *kontakion*, he sings of the Virgin in these words:

> The Virgin, not knowing man, gave birth to joy; the sorrow of our Ancestor is now overcome. The Uncreated is born, the Uncontainable is contained. Joy is manifested today, error is destroyed today. Nations, let us say: "Blessed are you, our newborn God, glory be to you."
>
> What mortal intelligence can explain your giving birth? How shall we call you, O glorious Mary? Through you, the Maker of creation has become flesh. "Hail," I will say to the Lamb; "Hail," I will shout to the Virgin. Nations, let us say: "Blessed are you, our newborn God, glory be to you."
>
> The Author of the Law has become flesh, subject to the Law; the eternal Son is born of the Virgin, the Creator of the universe is lying in a manger. He whom the Father generated without a mother, has become the son of the Virgin without a father. Nations, let us say: "Blessed are you, our newborn God, glory be to you."
>
> The choir of angels sings a hymn to you, O Mary, shining Mother who knew not man. Celebrate your Son fittingly with dances of joy: Hail, hope of your

---

5. This Christmas *kontakion* by Romanos the Melodist is made up of *oikos* or stanzas to be sung in the divine office, between the verses of the psalms.

servants; hail, protection of those who believe up-rightly! Nations, let us say: "Blessed are you, our new-born God, glory be to you."

O Virgin, the fruit of your womb, swaddled in the crèche, taught us to rejoice with you: living in your womb, he did not violate your virginity. The Incarnate Word appears, willingly made man, by a manner inexplicable. Nations, let us say: "Blessed are you, our newborn God, glory be to you."

The Virgin who gave birth to God was prefigured by the Ark, the means of conciliation for the world: it also held the urn and the manna and, through it, Israel was guided. We too sing a hymn to the Mother of God: "Blessed are you, our newborn God, glory be to you."[6]

These are the Marian themes contemplated by the saints; Saint Louis-Marie Grignion de Montfort uses different words to echo those of Romanos the Melodist:

God the Son descended into her virginal womb, as the New Adam into his terrestrial paradise, to take his pleasure there, and to work in secret the marvels of his grace.

God-made-Man found his liberty in seeing himself imprisoned in her womb. He made his omnipotence

6. Romanos the Melodist, *Inni* [Hymns], ed. G. Gharib (Rome: Edizioni Paoline, 1981), XV, 6, 8, 11, 13, 21, 24, pp. 190–193 (translation John A. Di Camillo).

shine forth in letting himself be carried by that humble maiden. He found his glory and his Father's in hiding his splendors from all creatures here below and revealing them to Mary only. He glorified his independence and his majesty, in depending on that sweet Virgin.[7]

Blessed Alberione's practical applications are quite compelling. He encourages us not to limit our meditation on the manger to Christmas, but rather to extend that contemplation to the altar:

Why all this joy? All this gladness? This gladness has its source in the Incarnation of the Word, in the birth of the Savior. God became part of the human family, as the liturgy says: God in our family, and we in God's family, because the Son of God became man to raise man to God: "*Ut homo fieret Deus*" ("so that man might become God," says Saint Augustine). Our manger is the altar: it is here in particular that we encounter God and become part of the divine family. The altar is our manger, where Jesus is born for us. . . . Coming back to the family, all Christians should manifest their joy, joy that comes to them from the presence of God among us. "*Et cum hominibus conversatus est*" (Bar 3:38: "is at home with mortals").[8]

---

7. De Montfort, *True Devotion*, pt. I, sec. I, p. 9.
8. Alberione, *Per un rinnovamento*, 306.

Following the example of Jesus who let himself be guided and formed by his mother, we seek to model ourselves more and more after Mary, our mother and teacher.

The Holy Family

The pastoral attention Pope Francis devotes to the family is well known, and the post-synodal apostolic exhortation *Amoris Laetitia* is a concrete example of it. The profound meaning of this invaluable document, which attained special significance during the Jubilee Year of Mercy, is made clear in the very first paragraphs: "First, because it represents an invitation to Christian families to value the gifts of marriage and the family, and to persevere in a love strengthened by the virtues of generosity, commitment, fidelity and patience. Second, because it seeks to encourage everyone to be a sign of mercy and closeness wherever family life remains imperfect or lacks peace and joy."[9]

The month of December, so dear to the faithful because of the solemnities of the Immaculate Conception of Mary and the Nativity of Jesus, closes with the feast of

---

9. Francis, Post-Synodal Apostolic Exhortation *Amoris Laetitia*, March 19, 2016, no. 5, https://w2.vatican.va/content/dam/frances-co/pdf/apost_exhortations/documents/papa-francesco_esortazione-ap_20160319_amoris-laetitia_en.pdf.

the Holy Family. This celebration makes the prayer to the Holy Family at the conclusion of the document *Amoris Laetitia* particularly fitting and relevant:

> Jesus, Mary, and Joseph,
> in you we contemplate
> the splendor of true love;
> to you we turn with trust.
>
> Holy Family of Nazareth,
> grant that our families too
> may be places of communion and prayer,
> authentic schools of the Gospel
> and small domestic churches.
>
> Holy Family of Nazareth,
> may families never again experience
> violence, rejection, and division;
> may all who have been hurt or scandalized
> find ready comfort and healing.
>
> Holy Family of Nazareth,
> make us once more mindful
> of the sacredness and inviolability of the family,
> and its beauty in God's plan.
>
> Jesus, Mary, and Joseph,
> Graciously hear our prayer. Amen.[10]

Regarding the relationship among the members of the Holy Family of Nazareth, Pope Francis contemplates

---

10. Ibid., no. 325.

the "splendor of true love," the secret of which is "full of the fragrance of family,"[11] and in the concluding prayer he opens three paths for our prayer:

a) the first is proactive: the Pope invites us to ask the family of Nazareth to make all families of this world "places of communion," true cenacles of prayer that become "authentic schools of the Gospel" and "small domestic churches";

b) the second encourages us to pray that no family experiences "episodes of violence, rejection and division," and that, when human weakness is the cause of harmful events, timely interventions of comfort and healing may occur;

c) the third concerns the universal awareness "of the sacredness and inviolability of the family," previously emphasized by Paul VI in his homily at the Basilica of the Annunciation in Nazareth on January 5, 1964.

Awareness of this remains absolutely foundational for a right understanding of the family: only within this perspective is it possible to appreciate the natural role of the family in the social order, its noble vocation, and "its beauty in God's plan."

Jesus, Mary, and Joseph,
Graciously hear our prayer!

---

11. Ibid., no. 65.

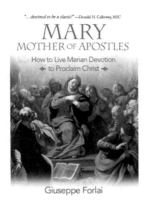

"...*destined to be a classic!*" —Donald H. Calloway, MIC

MARY
MOTHER OF APOSTLES

How to Live Marian Devotion
to Proclaim Christ

Giuseppe Forlai

Mary, Mother of the Apostles
How to Live Marian Devotion to Proclaim Christ

By Giuseppe Forlai

Father Forlai leads the reader into a deeper love for Our Lady, drawing on the thought of Saint Louis de Montfort, Saint John Paul II, and Blessed James Alberione. Discover how Marian devotion and consecration are paths to personal holiness and effective evangelization.

0-8198-4974-X
$12.95
128 pages

BOOKS & MEDIA

A mission of the Daughters of St. Paul

As apostles of Jesus Christ, evangelizing today's world:

We are CALLED to holiness
by God's living Word and Eucharist.

We COMMUNICATE the Gospel message
through our lives and through all
available forms of media.

We SERVE the Church
by responding to the hopes and needs
of all people with the Word of God,
in the spirit of St. Paul.

For more information visit us at
www.pauline.org.

BOOKS & MEDIA

The Daughters of St. Paul operate book and media centers at
the following addresses. Visit, call, or write the one nearest you
today, or find us at www.paulinestore.org.

CALIFORNIA
3908 Sepulveda Blvd, Culver City, CA 90230   310-397-8676
3250 Middlefield Road, Menlo Park, CA 94025   650-562-7060

FLORIDA
145 S.W. 107th Avenue, Miami, FL 33174   305-559-6715

HAWAII
1143 Bishop Street, Honolulu, HI 96813   808-521-2731

ILLINOIS
172 North Michigan Avenue, Chicago, IL 60601   312-346-4228

LOUISIANA
4403 Veterans Memorial Blvd, Metairie, LA 70006   504-887-7631

MASSACHUSETTS
885 Providence Hwy, Dedham, MA 02026   781-326-5385

MISSOURI
9804 Watson Road, St. Louis, MO 63126   314-965-3512

NEW YORK
115 E. 29th Street, New York City, NY 10016   212-754-1110

SOUTH CAROLINA
243 King Street, Charleston, SC 29401   843-577-0175

TEXAS
No book center; for parish exhibits or outreach evangelization, contact:
210-569-0500, or SanAntonio@paulinemedia.com, or P.O. Box 761416,
San Antonio, TX 78245

VIRGINIA
1025 King Street, Alexandria, VA 22314   703-549-3806

CANADA
3022 Dufferin Street, Toronto, ON M6B 3T5   416-781-9131